# KORAN BOLDEN

National Youth Speaker & Entrepreneur

# ROCK PAPER SCISSORS

### 3 SECRETS TO HOW YOUR FAILURES CAN MAKE YOU
## FAMOUS

Business Strategy for Millennials

Dream Success
www.KoranBolden.com

To one of the best social change agents I know, I declare that 2015 is the year of increase. Your students will excell in all areas of life as they see you lead by example. 2015 is your year to excellence. Dream Big!

**Rock, Paper, Scissors**

Printed in the United States by
Mira Digital Publishing
Chesterfield, Missouri 63005

# DEDICATION

I would like to dedicate this book to the memory of Anthony Bolden, Matthew Brown, Robert Henry Jr., and Martha Christmas. These four heroes were major influences in my life and helped to cultivate me into a man of success. Sadly, they passed before the results sprouted. Their life lessons and legacy will live on through me. I miss them all dearly.

# CONTENTS

"Koran Bolden is that shining example for youth today. His dedication to make a difference in the lives of others is like no other. He's dynamic, he's passionate, he leads with tenacity and humility and he's guided by an amazing set of core values. Lessons all of us can benefit from. I was on the edge of my seat watching him tell his story. You will be too, as you read "Rock, Paper, Scissors."

- Susan Goss-Brown, Vice President
Banana Republic Stores-Domestic

"I had the great pleasure of scouting Koran Bolden as a youth ambassador for our Walgreens Expressions Challenge program where we encourage students to make healthy life choices through various forms of positive self expression. Koran was not only a tremendous asset to the team as a spokesperson for our school tour, he also helped us develop relevant content and strategies to expand our Walgreens outreach initiative to students who need it the most."

- Peggy Austin, President
GoldStar Communications/Walgreens Expressions Challenge

"Koran is committed to establishing positive opportunities for young people in the community. He utilizes his musical talents and motivational speaking skills to reach and inspire individuals who find themselves without hope. Street Dreamz will not only add value to any organization's efforts, but is a positive and effective way to influence our youth."

- Melba R. Moore, Commissioner of Health
City of St. Louis Department of Health

"When we invited Koran Bolden to speak at our annual Field Leadership Conference we knew we were getting a loyal customer and committed community activist; someone who could inspire our store managers. However, we didn't realize we were also getting one of the most promising young motivational speakers working today; a future star of TED with a message perfect for engaging today's Millennial workforce. Koran was a highlight of our conference bringing 1,000 leaders from around the world, first to tears, then to their feet for a standing ovation!"

- Dan Leavitt, Sr. Manager
Banana Republic Learning & Development

"As a youth development professional, I know that there are very few people who are able to connect with youth the way Koran Bolden does. He truly understands the value of positive thinking, education, hard work, determination and integrity and he incorporates these values into his work. He is a visionary who knows that our communities can only be as strong as our children and I strongly endorse Koran Bolden and the work he is doing to build strong children."

- Jody J. Squires Ph.D, Urban Youth Development Specialist
University Of Missouri Extension

"I have listened to many speakers with the hopes of engaging and connecting with youth. Some do it well and others do it with great passion, ease and impact. Koran has the ability of connecting and reaching young people in a meaningful way and inspires them to challenge themselves. The message he shares not only inspires, it also challenges them to think and we know just thinking is the biggest hurdle."

- Diana Wilhold, Director, BJC HealthCare
School Outreach and Youth Development

"Koran Bolden's TEDx talk was a well thought out translation of one's responsibilities in life condensed down to a children's game 'Rock, Paper, Scissors'. His high energy and core belief in the message spoke to an enraptured audience. Koran held everyone in his alternating 'Rock, Paper, Scissor' shaped hand throughout this engaging talk. Great Job!"

- Steve Sommers, Curator
TEDxGatewayArch

"I enthusiastically endorse Mr. Koran Bolden and his company Street Dreamz Artist Development Center. In my work with him over the past two years, I have been impressed with him as a leader in his industry and role model for the young people he works with. Koran is an innovative thinker who takes time to mentor and empower youth on a daily basis. In working with Koran he has not only impacted individual students in my school, rather he has helped to transform our school culture through the creative arts."

- Gary Spiller, Principal at McCluer High School
Ferguson-Florissant School District

"Koran Bolden is one of the most dynamic young men I've had the privilege of meeting over the course of a lengthy professional career. He is not only articulate and intelligent, but has a vision, purpose, message and conviction. He is an outstanding speaker who knows how to reach the younger generation and convey his personal story of perseverance, success and conviction."

- Christi Griffin, Founder/President
The Ethics Project

"Koran Bolden is a true inspiration and thought leader. By sharing his personal journey with the Banana Republic team, he provides tremendous motivation to seize your potential by utilizing his Rock Paper Scissors philosophy. You never know how your interactions will affect others and Koran's vision gave our team the inspiration to live up to our promise to Do More."

- Curtis Pinkerton, Regional Community Leader
Banana Republic

"Koran has tremendous communication skills, is extremely organized, reliable and talented. Koran can work independently and is able to follow through to ensure that the job gets done. He accomplishes these tasks with great initiative and enthusiasm. His work with youth and our community make him an excellent candidate for leading and motivating others."

- Susan Kelly, Principal at Ferguson Middle
Ferguson-Florissant School District

"Both Koran and LaPortcia Bolden are ordinary people who have captured the essence of what it means to be extraordinary. When it comes to displaying leadership, sharing their talents with young people and taking on the complexities of the trials, troubles and tribulations of everyday life, each stand ready to help, support and provide whatever is necessary to turn the three T's into triumphs."

- Tony Neal, President/CEO
Educational Equity Consultants

"Koran believes in education and promoting healthy relationships through positive interaction. Because of his talents and willingness to share his knowledge with the community, he has impacted many lives in a positive and upward direction. Koran is continuously looking for new ways to improve and educate the community."

- Robin Foster, Student Affairs Coordinator
St. Louis Job Corps Center

"Koran is motivated, a positive role model for children and dedicated to making a difference within the community. His impact and influence on the youth in the community speaks to his outstanding performance as a leader."

- Shannon Woodcock, Executive Director
Delta Dental Health Theatre

"Not only does Mr. Bolden visit schools to empower, strengthen, and encourage students to dream big and stay in school, but he works to maintain that relationship with the school and students. His intentions of reaching out to schools and students to be a steward of his mission is clear and refreshing. We have greatly appreciated his visit, ongoing communications, and hard work to make a difference for St. Louis youth. I would highly recommend his visit to your school to empower your students as well!"

- Emily Turner, Principal at Lee-Hamilton Elementary
Ferguson-Florissant School District

## My Thank You Letter From The Heart

When I first started out on my journey to become an entrepreneur, the very first goal I made for myself was simple: wake up every day, and fly higher than I did the day before. To say the least, it worked! How could I have ever made it this far without the loving support of my beautiful wife, LaPortcia Bolden, along with my mother Adrianne, sister Cherie, nephew Brandon, and best friend Robby. They were the ones who believed in me with unfailing support, to step out in the deep to start my own business. To my son Koran Jr., and daughters Kailee and Tahlia, I wrote this book for you as an inheritance of wisdom. I want you to know how I struggled in life so that you won't have to make the same mistakes that I did. This is how the Bolden family will evolve and advance from one generation to the next.

Finally, to every person that joined me as a volunteer, advocate, or staff member, whether it was for a season or for a lifetime, your hard work, blood, sweat and tears allowed us to impact our city. Your courage to fight for what we believed in has inspired the masses to break beyond the limits of failure to live the life of an entrepreneur, the ultimate American Dream. The best is yet to come!

Yours Truly,

–President of Young America, Koran Bolden
Street Dreamz School of Business and Performing Arts

"Twenty years from now you will be more disappointed by the things that you didn't do than by the ones you did do. So throw off the bowlines. Sail away from the safe harbor. Catch the trade winds in your sails. Explore. Dream. Discover." -Mark Twain

# resilient |riˈzilyənt|

adjective
(of a substance or object) able to recoil or spring back into shape after bending, stretching, or being compressed. See note at **flexible** .
• (of a person or animal) able to withstand or recover quickly from difficult conditions : *the fish are* **resilient to** *most infections.*

# INTRODUCTION

"The two most important days of your life are the day you were
born and the day you find out why." -Mark Twain

## Street Dreamz Headquarters

It was 12 midnight, as I sat inside my recording studio in awe
of everything that was going on in my life at that time. In
under 3 years I have managed to conquer the statistics of
being just another young black male whose doctor once
prescribed with a dose of, "He will probably end up dead or
in jail," to becoming Mr. Verizon Wireless Everyday Hero
2013, a national youth motivational speaker, and a young
entrepreneur with a prestigious styled resume. As I stared at
my computer screen with just a few last sips of my Starbucks
hot carmel macchiato with double whipped cream, I started
to reflect on my previous life before opening my own
business called Street Dreamz Recording Studio & Party
Center.

Who would have ever thought that just 4 years ago I was on
the brink of a total meltdown. There were long days and
dreadful months where every room I walked in felt as if it
was closing in on me. My confidence was at an all time low
and my household was a complete wreck. Since I was the

type of person that measured my self-worth through money, achievement and performance, I decided to work an insane amount of overtime hours at my job to sustain the little bit of sanity that I had left. Every day I overworked myself to keep my mind busy to avoid dealing with the painful thoughts of living check to check, ducking and dodging the repo man, being behind on my rent, and all of the recent failures that haunted me. But in the end, my unwillingness to face my problems head on mixed with extreme busyness only made matters worse. I became a highly irritated workaholic who developed a low tolerance level for the slightest bit of displayed ignorance in thought or speech from others. I literally tried everything I could think of to shake the flood waves of negative thoughts, but nothing seemed to work. To make a long miserable story short, I was sinking and sinking fast.

### Snap Out Of It!

Then it happened! With the little bit of faith I had left, I decided that it was time to shake the dust off my shoulders and give life another try with everything I had in me. It was time to do an extreme mental makeover and there was no turning back. I immediately surrendered all of my thoughts to God All Mighty, and declared that nothing on this earth would stop my vision to be an advocate for social change and entrepreneurship, and the rest was history.

The first steps of action that led me to my big turnaround was to take a closer look at how I perceived failure. I spent hours upon hours transforming my mindset by listening to podcast and YouTube videos of the wealthiest entrepreneurs and success coaches in the world. After tons of studying, I have since discovered that the failures that once haunted me were actually working in my favor all along to make me famous. But not the fame you think of with tons of paparazzi crowding your every move and millions of screaming fans barricading your doorstep. I'm speaking of a fame that spreads so great that the reputation of your good works show up on the scene way before your physical body ever occupies the space. I am speaking of leaving a legacy where people talk about you long after you leave this earth from all the charitable contributions you've made to improve society. I'm talking about a life full of true purpose, happiness and total fulfillment!

## What Is Failure?

When most people think of the word failure, the worst thoughts seem to come to mind. To sum it up in simple terms, being a failure is synonymous with being deemed a **loser**. But let's set the record straight, just because you have *failed* at a task once or twice does not make you a *failure*. What makes you a *failure* is when you refuse to see the *privileged* learning opportunity after you have met face to face with the grips of failure. There is a quote by Babe Ruth that drives this point home clearly. It says, "Every strike brings me closer to the next home run."

As an entrepreneur who started out with nothing, I can surely tell you I have experienced more than my fair share of failures. At the moment failure occurs, some people describe a mental cloudiness hovering above them that literally makes them feel like crawling under a rock and dying as if they were never born. But how could we dare give up when the greatest champions the earth has ever birthed proclaim that failure was the secret sauce to success? Did we miss the memo? Why is it that one group of people experience failure and feel as if the world is coming to an end, and another group experience that same level of disappointment but manages to become even more empowered and successful than they did before adversity showed up?

I now welcome you into a life changing moment with countless stories of personal results that will teach you how to fall into group #2 that obtains a greater empowerment as they experience struggles. After all my research, I made an amazing discovery about the mindset and how humans process failure. The first discovery I made was that there were two different types of failure. The first type of failure is a negative impact failure. This is the type of failure a person experiences when they set a goal and doesn't put forth the adequate amount of effort and practice to achieve the goal. In the end, they live a life full of mediocrity and regret. Not because they failed, but because they made an attempt to achieve greatness without giving their all. Even if they win, they still lose because they didn't push their talent capabilities to a higher limit.

The second discovery I made involves those who experienced a positive impact from failure. These were people who decided that no matter if they win or lose, they were going to give it all they've got. These were the people who stayed in the house and worked on their craft while their colleagues were spending all their valuable time out partying with friends 24/7. These were people who were willing to sacrifice temporal pleasure and comfort just to experience the sizzling taste of success. Although this group of people experienced failure, they felt as if they still ultimately won because they made their great attempt to achieve success by giving their best efforts. This group had longer longevity in their careers.

### Perspective On Failure Chart

| Failure Type | Effort | Adversity | Results |
|---|---|---|---|
| **Negative Impact Failure** | Little to no effort | Didn't embrace failure and chose to quit | Low self-esteem and mediocrity |
| **Positive Impact Failure** | High amount of effort | Embraced failure and learned to recover quickly | High self-esteem and talents excelled |

There is so much more I have discovered, but before I give up the goodies, I want you to first understand that although I have endured much heartache and pain to share this story for the benefit of my readers, nothing in life will move unless you do. The stories I'm about to share can't help a person that's not willing to help themselves. Although I believe with all my heart that this book can help change your life for the better, you have to want change just as much as I want it for you. A great success coach by the name of Jim Rhone once said, "You can't hire other people to do your pushups for you." That means if you want to get results, *you*'re going to have to put in the work to obtain it. Always remember, a book is only as effective as the readers' willingness to put its principles in action. So let's begin.

# Enter At Your Own Risk

One hot summer, I decided to go hang out at the pool with a few under aged friends. The sign on the apartment complex pool clearly stated, *"Do Not Enter Without Adult Supervision Or Life Guard"*. Being the innocent curious genius child that I was at the time, I decided to influence my friends to join me for a few dips in the pool anyway. The only problem was, I couldn't swim! Shortly after my mischievous offer, my friends burst through the gate and immediately dove into the deep end. "Hey Koran, what are you waiting on, dive in with us!" they cheerfully shouted. Instead of declining their call to action and informing them that I couldn't swim, I stalled and decided to *play it safe* by sitting at the edge of the pool on the deep end and dangled my feet in the water.

Moments passed by while fear and embarrassment started to sink deep within me. I knew the time was coming for me to dive in and hopefully maneuver through the water like a pro or chicken out and reveal my inexperience of swimming. To make matters worse, the blistering heat from the sun beaming down upon my head mixed with my swimming insecurities started to make me feel a little nauseous and within seconds the next few moments of my life would be life changing.

With one simple slip of the hand, I accidentally fell in the pool with no adults or life guard to save me. Not knowing how to swim made me fall into a state of panic which made matters of me drowning even worse. "Help, Help!" I screamed as water started to overflow into my nostrils and lungs. My body became lifeless after the water started to slowly suffocate me from breathing as I fought for my last breaths of air. My promising childhood life flashed before my eyes and all I could think of was how I just made the biggest mistake of my life. "I have failed. My life is now over," I thought to myself.

## Have You Ever Felt Like You Were Drowning?

Have you ever been in a position where you felt like your life or dream was over? Have you ever been drowning in debt, failing in school, didn't get the promotion you desired, felt like bad things only happen to you, or felt like you always get the short end of the stick? I know exactly how you feel. Although my unforgettable day at the pool is my story of a literal drowning, life's failures can produce comparable results. Many times I have worked on big projects with major corporations and felt underprepared or overcommitted for the challenge that was before me. The stress from success can soon make it hard to properly execute, which leads to procrastination and indecision which when left unresolved can pressure you to allow your dream to slip away like I did in the pool that day. This truly feels like a place of no return. But failure doesn't have to be the end, for my near tragedy at the pool ends with a sigh of relief and a great lifelong lesson.

## Thank God For Friends

One of my friends who was an awesome swimmer observed me drowning and jumped in to save me. He literally pulled me out the water in the nick of time. "Why were you in the deep end of the pool if you knew you couldn't swim?" he asked in deep concern and frustration after catapulting my cold body onto the hard concrete deck. All I could do was shrug my shoulders and blink in amazement from all that just occurred. At that moment, I learned three valuable crash course lessons from the school of failure that I will share with you today.

## Lesson #1

The first is that there are warning signs all around us that inform us of the consequences of bad decision making. For me, the warning sign on the gate should have been my first clue that possible danger was ahead. I foolishly ignored the sign as if it didn't apply to me or my genius-ness and found myself in a world of trouble which almost resulted in me losing my life. If you desire to be successful in business, you must know how to properly read and adhere to the invisible warning signs that keep you from danger while simultaneously developing your inner intuitions that lead you to success.

This failure at the pool revealed to me the importance of developing an intuitive heart and mind in business that will amazingly improve your ability to judge when a good deal is on the table or if there is trouble ahead.

## Fast Talking Freddy

I remember a time when I was working in corporate America. One of my co-workers, who I will call Freddy for the sake of privacy, kept showing me how much money he made with live speed trading on the stock market. His excitement and enthusiasm felt electric as he kept showing me how much profit he made in just a few hours from trading online. He then proposed for me to join along in his get-rich-quick scheme by making a personal monetary investment with a **guarantee** that I could achieve the same results. Normally, I wouldn't have even given him an ear to listen, but I was in desperate need for some extra cash because I was behind on some bills. Unsurprisingly, the more I gave him my attention the more he began to fast talk and pressure me to buy in. By the way, when a person starts fast talking and applying pressure for you to make an immediate decision, those are definite *warning signs* that you are embarking on a bad deal.

Fast talking Freddy kept saying, "Come on Koran, let me make you some money man," but at the last minute before I completed the transition to invest I decided to follow my gut instinct and backed out the deal.

A few weeks later, I saw Freddy sitting at his desk with a facial expression filled with disappointment and frustration so I decided to ask if he was ok. He replied, "Not at all Koran. I just lost all of my money today in the stock market. This included my whole paycheck and my previous profits. I'm about to lose everything I have."

This is an extremely sad story and prime example of what I mean when I say look for the warning signs and always follow your gut. If there is no peace with your decision, do not move forward.

Whenever I'm in doubt on a situation I always reach down deep in prayer and follow my gut over all rational thinking. Ultimately, when your gut tells you not to do business with a person and you don't have a reason why not to do the deal, always follow intuitive guide above all. Follow the warning signs. You will thank me later!

## Lesson #2

The second lesson learned is that we will all inevitably make bad choices in life, but that's why it is extremely important for you to surround yourself with a support group of colleagues and mentors. They should be our second set of eyes when we have been blindsided by the devastating claws of failure.

The reason that I didn't drown that day at the pool was not because I didn't have enough friends there with me. The swimming pool was packed with people that day. The reason I didn't drown is because *one* of my friends was *alert* and knew how to do something that I couldn't do which was swim. There could have been 30 people at the pool that day but if none of them could swim, how would I have been saved from drowning? World thought leader on the subject of vulnerability Brene Brown says it perfectly when she was quoted saying, "Social media had given us this idea that we should all have a posse of friends when in reality, if we have one or two really good friends, we are lucky."

I hear so many arrogant young professionals brag about how many people they have in their phone list. But who cares if you have a million numbers in your contact list if none of them can help you. I would rather have five strong progressive relationships that I can foster and nurture over a lifetime than have 500 revolving door relationships in constant motion. It's not the quantity, it's all about quality that counts.

In life, we all should be constantly connecting with new friends that come from diverse backgrounds that have strengths in areas we are weak in. This is what opens the opportunity for us to make a strong collective impact on our community, because the truth is we all need each other to thrive and succeed.

## Stinking Thinking!

I remember in my younger days, I grew up watching the #1 children's show of all times called Sesame Street. Their easy to sing jingle and catchy tune to this day can still spark a lifetime of childhood memories for most of us. A few months ago I pondered on something very intriguing about one of the original characters on the show named Oscar.

Oscar the Grouch was introduced to the world as the puppet that lived inside the trash can on Sesame Street. In scene after scene, Big Bird and several other friends would express their thoughts with Oscar only to realize that by listening and asking Oscar for advice only left them worse off than before they came. To this day, I still can't figure out why Oscar was so mad when he lived on an amazing street that even the theme song proclaims that everybody wants to get to.

Sunny Day
Sweepin' the clouds away
On my way to where the air is sweet

Can you tell me how to get,
How to get to Sesame Street

Come and play
Everything's A-OK
Friendly neighbors there
That's where we meet

Can you tell me how to get
How to get to Sesame Street

Although we may not have the full answer as to why Oscar was such a grouch, some of us are just like Oscar when it comes to us meeting new people and thinking outside the box. If I would view this from a business perspective, Oscar had the opportunity to become a great businessman. He had all the resources and people around him that would have been glad to support his vision and even helped his trash collecting business grow, but instead he chose to spend the majority of his time complaining and being prideful instead of asking for help. Oscar essentially became his own worst enemy. He let his current lifestyle of living in a garbage dump rob him of a promising happy filled future on Sesame Street.

You may laugh at this analogy, but this is truly no laughing matter at all. Millions of us are living our life everyday just like Oscar the Grouch and we don't even know it. We sit around and complain about our current problems so much to the point that we don't even realize that there are blessings right within our everyday reach and we are too blind to take notice.

Had I been in Oscar's shoes, I would have took yesterday's setbacks and used them as today's comeback by becoming a world class business owner in the garbage business. If he would have just stopped complaining and opened his eyes, Oscar would have seen that he had a celebrity friend named Big Bird whom everybody loved. He could have asked him to become the vice-president of the community engagement department to his new garbage business especially since Big Bird possessed great relationships with the townspeople. He even had a mastermind accountant by the name of Count Dracula who would have been more than happy to file his taxes for him for free. But Oscar was too busy meditating on the problems instead of focusing on solutions. Success and happiness was right outside his comfort zone and in his face all along, but Oscar refused to ask for help and unfortunately became complacent and stuck in his ways. His pride stopped him from ever reaching for higher horizons and the story ends every episode with Oscar remaining a grouch, defeated in a trash can his entire career.

## Finding New Friends

For most of us, adding new people to our circle is a hard thing to ask because it's really difficult to trust people these days. We all have experienced our fair share of the backstabbing ex-best friends or co-workers who played the scandalous office politics game on us, but so what! Life goes on. If they are speaking negatively about you and you found out, they just did you a favor. They should have been gone a long time ago. They don't deserve a good friend like you in the first place.

If you don't let go and move forward, you will take that toxic wasteful thinking into your next relationship, marriage, or business partnership just like Oscar. You will become so suspicious, critical, and fault finding that you will diminish every new opportunity to meet the new people that will come into your life that have no intentions of ever backstabbing.

Yes, good friends are hard to come by and when you find them you will have to expose yourself to a certain level of vulnerability and possibly being hurt again. But remember that you have to dig deep for diamonds and having a good support of friends is truly priceless.

Your support group should be there to hold you accountable and make sure you're moving towards your goals. They also should be alert and ready to pull you out the pool when you accidentally slip in from ignorance, arrogance, or exhaustion. It's time to increase your reach. Step outside of your comfort zone and make it a priority to meet some new people this week.

---

"You can never expect Oscar to stop being a grouch until you first convince him to step outside his trash can." -Koran Bolden

---

## Lesson #3

People are only afraid of what they cannot control or understand. The reason I had a near death experience is because I never took the time to educate myself on how to swim. I sunk from a lack of education. If I had only taken the time to learn how to swim by a *professional swimmer*, even if I made the mistake and slipped in the pool I still would have been able to stay afloat. This is one of the main reasons why I am writing this book as well. I have seen too many businesses fail. I have seen too many people tell me their brilliant ideas and a year later they are still in the same boat they were in when I met them or worse. This does not have to be you and I righteously declare that it will not be you.

I have made way too many mistakes in life to sit back and let you fall in the same business traps as me. I humbly, but unapologetically, consider myself a professional when it comes to community empowerment and self branding. If you have a strong desire to give back to your community or re-invent yourself in the highest magnitude, I strongly advise you to follow my instructions closely and you will see these principals work in your life.

## Summary

Hopefully by now, you have somewhat of a basic idea of how your failures are really setting you up for an amazing life depending on your perspective. This is not a self help book, but rather a book that will give you a jumpstart or spark to your already existing power supply.

To bring this introduction to a close I want you to know that you have a great flame burning within you to accomplish the greatest achievements known to mankind. From the day you were born, God thought to perfectly create a vessel that would perform wonderful deeds to encourage the masses to fulfill their mission here on earth.

My job is not to give you a vision or to ask you to follow in my footsteps because you have your own destiny for greatness inside you already. You are already equipped with the potential to change the world. My job is to help you activate it. Just like a car battery, sometimes life drains us of all our power with all its negativity and all we need is a quick jumpstart to get back on the road. As you read every page in this book, picture me hooking up my jumper cable of success to help you to restart your engine. The interesting part about a battery is that they all have a negative and positive charge. That represents the good and the bad experiences in life that we all must face. They are both working together to get a car moving. I am officially plugging my jumper cables onto your battery to help start your engine!

# CHAPTER 1
# "THE SECRET SAUCE FORMULA"

"I am not a product of my circumstances. I am a product of my decisions." -Stephen Covey

Since we previously discussed how your failures can be a great benefit to you if you learn from them, I now want to discuss how you can avoid making some of these mistakes as well. Trust me when I say that you don't have to touch the stove to truly know if it's hot or not. Let's begin.

## Rock Paper Scissors

I would now like to introduce you to the three building blocks needed to succeed. This three-step philosophy entitled Rock, Paper, Scissors totally revolutionized the way I process goal setting. When applied in determining the failing points in your decision making, you will quickly discover where you failed and why. Knowing where you failed will properly help you recover quickly from your mistakes and get you right back onto the racetrack to fulfilling your dreams. Here is what each word represents.

## 1. Rock- Believe

"Whether you think you can or think you can't,
either way you're right!" -Henry Ford

One day, two psychologists got together to study the impact belief had on athletes' mindset and physical performance. In their experiment they asked 12 sets of arm wrestlers to face an opponent in a single arm wrestling match. They first measured their physical strength then paired each arm wrestler with an opponent who was a total opposite in strength.

They then escorted both arm wrestlers in separate rooms and began to reveal information about the opponent they would face. The only catch is that they told the arm wrestler who was weaker in physical strength that he was significantly stronger than the opponent that he was about to face, and they told the arm wrestler with stronger physical strength that he was significantly weaker than the opponent he was about to face. After the study was concluded, the results were shocking. Ten out of 12 times, the arm wrestler who was weaker in strength defeated the opponent who was actually stronger in man power. Why? Because what you believe has a big impact on your performance. What I get from this study is that you can be fully capable of winning in life and still lose, but on the flip side you can be physically incapable of winning, and still win. It all ultimately comes down to your belief system.

So now, my question to you is what do you currently believe about yourself? Do you believe you deserve the best or the worst life has to offer?

Your belief system is the single most important driving force to building confidence. Our confidence and self esteem is compiled of who we currently are and how close we are to where we eventually want to be. The closer we are to achieving our dreams the more confident we become. The further we are from achieving our dreams, the more discouraged we become.

If we are honest, we all can admit that we have picked up some destructive beliefs in life whether through lack of education and opportunity, imposed beliefs by our parents, family and friends, through the media or through socialization. It's extremely important for me to show you how to properly identify these self limiting beliefs when they arise because without this understanding you are like a safari jeep stuck in the mud going absolutely nowhere. I can assure you that there is not one single person that lived on this earth who changed the world without an extreme high level of confidence running through their veins. Determining what you believe will help give you a keen sense of hope and clarity that will help you develop the highest level of self esteem enabling you to make great decisions that lead you to ultimate levels of success.

## 2. Paper- Write it Down

"Either write something worth reading or do something worth writing." -Benjamin Franklin

I cannot stress enough the importance of constantly writing your big idea on paper. Some like to write their goals as a list. Some draw floor plans of what their future business will look like, and some simply cut out their favorite house, cars, and celebrities they admire out of a recent magazine and put it on a vision board. Whatever your preference, before you make your first move, please put it on paper and make sure you dream extremely big. This technique has resulted in me partnering with Gap Inc., Banana Republic, Verizon Wireless, and being the spokesperson for the Walgreens Expression Challenge. Not too bad for a first time business owner who started with no contacts in his phone just 3 years ago huh?

### Street Dreamz Recording Studio

When I first got the vision to open my own recording studio, I was so excited that I wrote my first short business plan and floor design on a napkin. (Please don't judge me. I was so excited to write down my dream and that's all I had at the moment!)

When that big idea hits, stop whatever you're doing and take the time to write it down. If you're not responsible enough to write your God-given idea down, it may be given to someone else who is willing to at least take the time to write it down on paper.

Plus, normally when I try to rely on my memory to retrieve an idea that I procrastinated in writing down, I later come to

4

realize that I can't remember what I was given. That idea has now been given to someone else.

Please don't get caught up in making up excuses by saying that you don't know how to write a business plan. I didn't either. Just get started. Scribble it, write it, sing it, yell it, record it on your phone. Do whatever you have to. Just make sure you write it down. You never know who may be willing to fund your big idea after reading it on paper. I know that for a fact. Someone once wrote me a check for over $15,000 after seeing a plan I was working on. Later on I will definitely share how that happened for me and how it can happen for you later in the book. So stay tuned.

What I will say is PLEASE save yourself the embarrassment of talking to potential funders and mentors without having it printed on paper in a simple format. One business rule of thumb is that if you don't write it down, it never happened and never will.

## 3. Scissors- Focus

"Take up one idea. Make that one idea your life--think of it, dream of it, live on that idea. Let the brain, muscles, nerves, every part of your body, be full of that idea, and just leave every other idea alone. This is the way to success." -Swami Vivekananda

Let me be very blunt when I say this. Highly talented young professionals and entrepreneurs have one thing in common, and if you don't get this one thing under control you are destined to fail indefinitely. Please listen closely to the next sentence you're about to read and then read it again. *All things are possible, but you can't possibly do all things.*

Let me clarify.

Have you ever seen a squirrel sitting in the middle of the road while you were driving? As you start to approach him you begin to tap your brakes to give him some time to figure out which way he wants to go, but as you get closer you begin to notice that instead of him moving out the way to avoid getting run over, he gives you a blank stare as if he can't make up his mind. You then begin to slow up even more, noticing that you're about to run him over and at the last minute he panics and runs back and forth in the middle of the street trying to decide if he should take a risk and reach his original desired destination across the street or go back to where he first started. Then, in the last few seconds before almost getting ran over he finally decides to go back to his original starting point because he couldn't get focused on the one task which was to move ahead.

I'm sorry to admit it but this is the life of the everyday entrepreneur. We have so many talents and ideas that we become easily distracted, and when it's time to move forward and adversity comes our way we often run back to our comfort zone area.

If you try to do it all, you will become the jack-of-all trades but a master of none. Successful people that break away from achieving average results have understood the power of one focus. They have plenty of ideas that flood their mind every day, but they understand that it's impossible to effectively complete them all. It's time to take control over your success life and pick one main goal and give it all you've got. After all, if you really believe like you say you do in your dream, why not put all your eggs in one basket?

---

"We have to continually be jumping off cliffs and developing our wings on the way down." -Kurt Vonnegut

---

## My Exhortation

Follow your dreams. Follow your passion. Things may not happen the way you want them to happen, but focus will guide you to the right destination with less headache, frustration, discouragement, and extra stress that you don't need while you walk this journey of self discovery.

Whenever I ask an unfocused person with a visionary mindset what's new, they always tell me more than three main objectives that they are trying to achieve at the same time. I immediately become disengaged in the conversation because I know that their probability for success is slim to none.

What's your big idea? What's that one thing that you love to do that even if you didn't get paid for it you would still do it? What makes your eyes light up when you talk about it? What do you feel like your gift is to the world? What makes you lose track of time when you're doing it?

Now that you have your **Rock** and **Paper** established, I implore you to pick up your *Scissors* and cut away everything off your plate that doesn't align with what you believe or wrote down. Then work diligently at it until you get the job done! Desire to be laser sharp focused. Otherwise, you're just wasting your time, running back and forth to your starting point like the squirrel in the middle of the road.

## Why 2 Out Of 3 Won't Get The Job Done

One of the greatest pet peeves of mine is when I hear
mentors loosely tell their mentee that they have so much
potential to succeed. The word potential is defined as one's
capacity to *eventually* become or develop into in the future.
The reason I cringe at the word potential is because it gives
off the assumption that one has an infinite amount of time to
put their best foot forward. But the truth is that you don't
have to wait until tomorrow to believe that you're great
because you already are! You were great from the first day
God conceived you in his mind.

"Then God said. "Let us make mankind in our image, in our
likeness, so that they may rule over the fish in the sea and the birds
in the sky, over the livestock, and all the wild animals, and over all
the creatures that move along the ground." -Genesis 1:26

I'm sorry folks, but it's so time out for potential. Life is too
short and tomorrow is not promised. Just visit the local grave
yard and you will find thousands of people that took that
same potential to the grave with them because they thought
they had more time. This is a great falsehood. There has to
be a certain level of grit, desperation and urgency to obtain
tangible results. We have to learn to walk, talk, and live as if
our prayers are answered and our dreams already achieved.

The chart on the next page will help you identify your current
decision making pitfalls and where there may be room for
improvement. It's best to have your Rock, Paper, and
Scissors to increase your probability of success. Here is
what happens to business people who only have 2 out of 3.

| Primary Strength | Secondary Strength | Likely Reasons Why You Fail |
|---|---|---|
| Rock | Rock | A true workaholic who has nothing to show for their labor. They talk passionately about their dreams a lot, but that's about all you will get from them. |
| Rock | Paper | Lacks focus and normally has too many ideas on their plate to effectively complete any of them. Often complains of burnout and extreme fatigue. |
| Rock | Scissors | Doesn't have a blueprint and has feelings of being lost. They take 1 step forward but 2 steps backwards. |
| Paper | Paper | Needs all the facts before they make a move. So focused on not making the wrong move that they end up making no moves at all. |
| Paper | Scissors | This person walks by sight and not by faith. When God gives them a big vision, they write it down but immediately become discouraged by their current lack of resources, finances, and staffing capabilities to complete the mission. They hopelessly throw in the towel. |
| Scissors | Scissors | This is the person who helps everybody but often has a hard time helping themselves. They plug into everybody's vision except the one God gave them. Their ability to get the job done has them in high demand for recruitment from others. Their biggest downfall is not knowing when to say no to other people's requests. |

## The Visualization Challenge

I propose for you to read this book with a partner that's on the same pursuit for success and happiness as yourself. Set a time everyday to reflect on the chapters and share personal insights you received as you flip through each page.

Finally, to engage you into a quick visualization technique I use, I would like for you to take the next 15 minutes and think about what you want to achieve in life more than anything else. Maybe you want to be the first person to graduate from high school or college in your family. Maybe you want to save $1000 for an emergency fund to be prepared for unexpected tragedies. It could be that you want to make new friends, spend more time with your family, go on a dream vacation out of the country, or to make $5000 more than you did last year.

Whatever you imagine, all I ask is that you select a goal that you want for your life, and not the goals that other people want for your life. Then write down 10 healthy habits and/or ideas that you have come up with that will support you achieving your goal. For example, if you want to get a raise, one of your goals may be to come in early and leave late. You may decide to prepare your clothes the night before to avoid accumulating unnecessary tardiness on your record. After you're finished, fill out your name, today's date, what you're desiring, and sign the check to make a bold statement that you are now the true CEO of your future. I look forward to hearing all the success stories that come from your journey. Please email me your victories as they come, as often as you like. The Best Is Yet To Come!

success@KoranBolden.com

## Supporting Habits Needed To Reach Your Goals!

1._____          6._____

2._____          7._____

3._____          8._____

4._____          9._____

5._____          10._____

## Please Fill Out And Sign Below

---------------------------------------------------------------------

| | 1936 |
|---|---|
| | DATE |
| PAY TO THE ORDER OF _____ | $ [        ] |
| _____ DOLLARS | 🔒 |
| FOR _____ | |

⑈000000186⑈ 000000529⑈ 1000

# CHAPTER 2
# BECOMING A VISIONARY

---

"If you are not willing to risk the usual,
you will have to settle for the ordinary." -Jim Rohn

---

One simple but clear definition of a visionary reads like this: a person with original ideas about what the future will or *could* be like. Please notice emphasis on the word could. The could refers to those who never put their plans into action. As a visionary myself, seeing the vision is definitely the easy part. Just the thought of talking about your ideas to others can put you in a euphoric high with plenty of goose bumps to prove it. But after that emotional high comes down, you may feel like you have hit a brick wall. Sadly, this is the part where a majority of those with a dream will quit. They know *what* they want to do, they know *when* they want to do it, they may even know *where* they want to do it. They just don't know *how* to do it. As a heads up, these feelings are completely normal. To make sure your vision doesn't come to a halting stop, here are five key pointers that will help add fuel to your fire the next time you become a little hesitant about moving forward.

---

## Key 1# Your Vision Has To Be Bigger Than You

Last March, I was honored to have been nominated for the Promoting Teen Excellence award by Saint Louis Connect Care and former St. Louis City Tax Collector Michael McMillan. I was one of four recipients that night who was being honored for the commitment to social change in the community. But little did I know until I was escorted to my seat that I was going to be on the same award ticket as Judge Jimmie Edwards, Dr. James Whittico, and baseball hall of famer Lou Brock. Knowing that I was sitting at such a high ranking table, I decided to ask as many questions as I could at this once in a lifetime opportunity.

The opportunity to spark up a conversation with Lou Brock was available, and I asked him how was he able to endure the pain of being an African American baseball player who was literally called all types of racially discriminating names during and after his baseball games in times of color segregation. He looked at me with a look that was serious but distinct as the next few lines of heroism proceeded from his mouth. He said,

*"The only way I was able to push through the hateful chants of an immature world that didn't approve of me because of the color of my skin was to have a mission bigger than myself. Every time I went to bat and people chanted*

*negative words filled with hatred and vulgarity, I decided that I wouldn't take it personal. I knew I was fulfilling a bigger purpose. I let those words run down my back and I continued to stay focused thinking that I had to endure these current pains of adversity so that other African American players could have the opportunity to play in the future."*

In essence, what Lou Brock was saying is that he was willing to sacrifice the temptation of responding back in anger or quitting because he was commissioned with the *privilege* in life to be a trailblazer for others. This along with being an amazing baseball player is why Lou Brock has been inducted in the Baseball Hall of Fame. Lou Brock was willing to die, so that others could live. The Rock Paper Scissors method is just that to the core. You can only achieve something like that through having a one focus mindset.

## Key #2 Discipline Your Disappointments

One major key to my road of success is I have *learned* to master the art of disciplining my disappointments *quickly* after failure. This can often become the major difference maker between those who acquire hit and miss luck with success, and those who enter the champions realm of success by focusing on developing a deep level of consistency in their craft. Michael Jordan, one of the greatest basketball players who ever lived once said...

"I've missed more than 9000 shots in my career. I've lost almost 300 games. Twenty six times, I've been trusted to take the game winning shot and missed. I've failed over and over and over again in life. And that's why I succeed."

See, contrary to what most believe, true success comes from evaluating lessons learned after experiencing loss. Winners don't see temporary loss as indefinite failure, they see loss as a real time feedback indicator of room for improvement.

## Not Sure What Disappointment Sounds Like?

A person who has been deeply hurt by disappointment may say something like this...

### Disappointment Example A

"I can't believe Tom didn't come through on his promise. At this point in my life, I refuse to ask anybody to help me ever again. I can't believe I allowed myself to be vulnerable. I have been lied to and let down by so many people that I will never let my guard down by asking for help from others ever again!"

### Disappointment Example B

"Why is it that every time somebody needs a helping hand, I run to their rescue and bail them out of trouble even if that means giving my last, but when I need the slightest bit of help on my end, I get the cold shoulder and help is nowhere in sight?"

### Disappointment Example C

Laura the Co-Worker: Hey Sherry, a new position just became available that I think would be perfect for you. You have the credentials and have been working here for a long time. There wouldn't be a better person than you to get that new promotion.

Sherry: Thank you for the compliment, but I don't know if I really want to apply. I have a lot on my plate right now and a new position means new responsibilities that I'm not sure if I could handle at this moment. Besides, the last time I applied, a new employee who was a master at office politics got the position instead of me. I think I will pass for now. Maybe next year.

## It's Time To Come Out The Shell

In example C, Sherry had a valid reason for not having interest in taking the new position. If you honestly know that you have reached the max in your responsibilities, taking on more is the wrong choice. If you take on too many responsibilities you will become ineffective and of no good use to anyone and will eventually self destruct. However, the indication that Sherry's statement was driven by a limiting belief and disappointment is because after she stated her reason for not applying due to too much on her plate, she then justified and complained about her bitterness with the office politics that prevented her from receiving a promotion the last time she applied. Bitterness and complaining is a sure indicator of a person who is holding on to a limiting belief.

## What is Disappointment?

Disappointment is defined as being sad or displeased because someone or something has failed to fulfill one's hopes or expectations. If you or someone you know has ever made a statement like the examples above, it's highly likely that you are still holding on to heavy baggage. I have honestly stated all three of the disappointment examples above many times in my life but I have learned that if I want to achieve the extraordinary, I must break past yesterday's let downs. This is why you have never heard of an ordinary person achieving anything great because in order to be great you must be willing to take risks. And the biggest risk most people will face is the fear of disappointment, rejection and being told no. Why? As humans we all want to be well liked, respected, and to belong. When somebody or external circumstances violate our expectations, we tend to shy away like a turtle that gets hit and hides in his shell. The only way the turtle will come back out is if he feels safe and unthreatened. However champions fly at a higher altitude than this. We are willing to stick our necks out on the line to win big.

There have been many people that have made superficial promises to help me and my business and never came through. I must admit, my first thought was to play it safe and never ask for help again, but playing it safe just won't cut it. The business world is not for the faint at heart, it's for the fearless!

### Key #3 Take Full Accountability For Your Actions

---

"They say what doesn't kill you makes you stronger, but I say what doesn't make you stronger will kill you. There is no such thing as passive decision making." -Koran Bolden

---

### Power Of Attorney

Power of attorney is a term used when a person other than yourself is assigned to make decisions over your life including but not limited to your health and financial estates, when you're severely sick or not in a healthy state of mind to make decisions on your own. The use of power of attorney should only be given to somebody who has your best interest in heart, but sadly that's not always the case. The person with power of attorney has the legal right to sign legal documents on your behalf, depositing and withdrawing money from your bank account, and even has the power to pull the plug on you while you're on life support if your vital signs aren't showing any improvement with your health status.

Some people think that this process only happens when you are severely sick or on your death bed, but the power of attorney can be live and in full effect all throughout your life and some are too naive to recognize it. Whether you know it or not, life waits for no one. Either you're going to make good decisions and tell the world who you are, or they are going to use the power of attorney and make decisions for you without your consent. You cannot afford any longer to sit down in the dumps about mistakes made in your past and give the mediocre world the power of attorney over your life because the world does not have your best interest at heart. Here is what happens if you think the choices of others won't affect you.

## In The Same Boat

Two men were out on the ocean in a boat. One of them began drilling in the bottom of the boat, and the other, aghast said "What are you doing? Stop drilling!"

And the first man replied: "It's all right. I'm only drilling on my side."

## Taking Full Ownership

"I have learned over the years that when one's mind is made up, this diminishes fear." -Rosa Parks

Not taking control over your life gives others the power of attorney to take control and drill holes in your boat of success. What's worse is that people don't mind sabotaging your property when they don't own it because they have nothing to lose. The main course of action that must be recognized is the fact that nobody has the power to make you sink but you, and that's only because you allowed it. The choices you previously made or allowed others to make for you have now resulted in either a life that is favorable to you achieving your dreams or not so much. There is no such thing as riding life in neutral gear. Either you are moving backward or forward. It is time to accept the fact that you may not be able to change your past, but that doesn't stop you from changing your future. You must accept 100% responsibility for your actions and confess that you no longer will give anybody the authority to have power of attorney over your life. That can only happen if you quit complaining and playing the blame game. Your mother, father, sister, brother, teachers, friendships, relationships, or boss does not have the power to make personal choices for you. Every mistake and successful decision you made was your choice. So choose from this moment forward that you will be on an intentional pursuit of knowledge and awareness to start making better decisions that will in turn produce better habits, which will in turn produce a happier quality of life for you and your family. Giving somebody else power of attorney could lead to that person pulling the plug on your dreams.

## Key #4 Stop Seeking Validation From Others

---

"If you ever want a for sure pathway to go the wrong way in life, ask for somebody else's opinion of you." -Koran Bolden

---

### Jenny Jones

I have learned in life that sometimes the people you want the most attention from have the capabilities of hurting you the most if you make them your main source for validation. There used to be a popular hit TV talk show called Jenny Jones. She was infamous for people coming on her show to blast an ex-bully that teased them in school. These people spent their whole life making drastic changes in order to prove something to the person that doubted or bullied them in school. They did everything from working out to pursuing high paid careers, to all kinds of extreme acts just to finally bring them on the show to say, "Look at me now." Most of them had blossomed into really successful people. They did a complete 180-degree transformation.

Yet, as the victim of the bully hit the stage with their new walk, talk and attitude, something happened. The ex bully trashed their new look as well, despite their transformation. The bully either still found something wrong, or confessed that they didn't even remember insulting them. "We were just kids, and that's what kids do," stated one bully as he spoke to the angry studio audience. But the truth is, he was right. People say things carelessly all the time and forget what they say. And if they have quickly forgotten what was said, why haven't you? Why do we still hold on and focus our time on the negative instead of focusing on the positive things said about us. You may be saying to yourself, "Nobody ever speaks positive things to me", well I now give you the permission to forgive yourself for not speaking life over yourself.

When you allow a bully, ex-friend, boyfriend, girlfriend or anybody else in the world to be the reason you have to prove something, your imagination becomes hostage to them. You make it to the top to prove them wrong, but in the end, they may never acknowledge your success. The truth is, if they don't care about you when you're down, why do you think they will care about you when you're happy and successful. Stop seeking validations from others and begin to find ways to build your self esteem and validate yourself. I will discuss forgiveness in more details in a later chapter as it is a necessity to living a healthy life.

## Key #5 Believe All Things Are Possible

---

"If we can send men to the moon, and surf the internet through an invisible signal, why in the world do we as humans think that anything is impossible?" -Koran Bolden

---

### Kid Solves Unsolvable Math Problem

A young college student was working hard in an upper-level math course for fear that he would be unable to pass. On the night before the final, he studied so long that he overslept the morning of the test.

When he ran into the classroom several minutes late, he found three equations written on the blackboard. The first two went rather easily, but the third one seemed impossible.

21

He worked frantically on it until — just ten minutes short of the deadline — he found a method that worked, and he finished the problems just as time was called.

The student turned in his test paper and left. That evening he received a phone call from his professor. "Do you realize what you did on the test today?" he shouted at the student.

"Oh, no," thought the student. I must not have gotten the problems right after all.

"You were only supposed to do the first two problems," the professor explained. "That last one was an example of an equation that mathematicians since Einstein have been trying to solve without success. I discussed it with the class before starting the test. And you just solved it!"

---

## Summary

The only reason you think you can't achieve greatness is because somebody told you that you couldn't. Like the Professor above, as humans we have the tendencies to pass down traditions from authority figures that say, "Don't question my authority, this is how it has always been done." But like the student above, he was never told that the problem was impossible so he believed that it was possible and therefore solved the problem. What person or limiting beliefs in your life have encouraged you to doubt your abilities to go to the next level in life? It's seriously time to go higher my friend. It's time to shift in a new gear!

After reading this chapter, take the next few moments and jot down some limiting beliefs you may have picked up along your journey. They can be big or small. We will discuss how to break through these barriers later.

_____

**Way To Go. Great Job!**

**You're Now On The Right Track!**

# CHAPTER 3
# READY, SET, GROW!

"Life is 10% what happens to me and 90% of how I react to it."
-Charles Swindoll

On a hot summer day in New Orleans, loud chants from a small group of spectators starting to gather could be heard from every apartment building overlooking the nearby playground. Fight! Fight! Fight! were the words being yelled as two best friends furiously arguing in the playground area were about to have a fist fight for absolutely no reason at all.

One half of the two young lads was of course yours truly, Mr. Koran Bolden, and the other was a kid named Tommy who was one of the brightest kids in the apartment complex. So your question at this moment might be, "Why in the world were you two about to fight?"

The fight and chants all started because I was known in this local community complex for street boxing. I had began to develop a love for boxing after watching clips of Iron Mike Tyson defeat his opponents in the boxing ring with unexplainable courage and sheer poise. So at the age of six, I had my first encounter and hunger for success which led me to a love for street boxing.

Unfortunately, my first passion for boxing was undisciplined and led me to fighting every kid in the area within a 10 mile radius that challenged me. My reputation for street fighting began to get so big that other kids in the area would have their cousins and friends from other towns spend the night at their house just to come fight me over the summer. But I had the heart of a champion. I defeated them all.

Being short in stature but lightning fast in speed, I defeated each of my opponents. I knew there was something different about me. I had a special gift that champions have which is the heart to sacrifice everything to win. Failure was not an option for me as I knocked down every opponent I fought. Not only did my confidence in boxing start to grow, but so did my level of respect and ego. I got to the point where I believed that no one could knock me down and I was completely unbeatable.

One of my best friends, Tommy, felt very safe and secure that he and I were best friends. After all, if your closest friend has gained a reputation in the area as little Iron Mike Tyson, your fear for having any bullying problems was not an issue for you to ponder on. The only problem was over time I started to let the talk of people calling me little Iron Mike go to my head. One hot summer day I would be tested in the area of leadership.

## The First Punch Thrown

This fist throwing scuffle started as I was playing on the playground. That particular day there was a slightly abnormal amount of older kids that were on the field, but no biggie to me! They all knew about my reputation and were the ones who gave me the Iron Mike moniker out of respect that I couldn't be beat. I guess the older kids wanted to be problematic and decided to start an instigating argument between me and Tommy which provoked us to fight one another. As egos flared around, side conversations started to conjure up and in seconds, out the clear blue sky we went from being best friends to enemies with our fists up.

A circle quickly formed around us, blocking and barricading us from leaving as the play yard felt as if it was spinning. The whole time I'm thinking to myself, "How did this happen so fast?" Deep down inside I wanted to stand up and be the better person and walk away, but the adrenaline rushing through my veins mixed with the chants from the crowd pulled me in an uncontrollable state of anger and competitiveness to knock him down and show him what I was truly made of.

Although I truly didn't want to fight my best friend at that moment, for some strange reason I think Tommy felt the same way. In fact, right before he threw the first punch at me he said, "Koran you may be my best friend and I really don't want to fight you, but I'm not about to back down and let you hit me first." At this point the crowd seemed even louder. Instigating chuckles, chants, and laughs were all I could hear as I was quickly being put in a trance-like zone which soon drowned out all outside voices in my mind as my friend grew eager in excitement and threw the first punch.

## Baaaaam! Oooooohhhhhh!

The crowd roared as the first punch sent a devastating blow to my head. I stumbled a bit and he threw another, and another. But little did he know that my experience and reputation from street fighting wasn't gained by pure luck. I had some real boxing skills.

I knew that when it came to street fighting that the person that does all the talking and screaming before the fight starts puts himself at a huge disadvantage. They work themselves up and tire themselves out before the real fighting begins. This gave me a huge advantage by staying calm, reserving my energy, and strategically assessing my fighting style needed to win.

## The Knock Out Punch

After his three big hits, he became tired and the rest was history. I delivered combo after combo and knocked Tommy out cold on his back as the crowd praised me and hugged me for another knock out.

After the fight was over people started to go back in their apartments and so did I. I remember thinking to myself, "What just happened"? I just fought and lost a really good friend of mine for no reason. "Where were all the people who started the fight," I wondered. They left me hanging cold. And even though they started the fight, I was the only person that would have to deal with the consequences and repercussions afterwards. As I sat in my room, I ultimately learned another good life lesson to my internal resume which is to always pick your battles wisely.

In life you may win the battle, but who cares if you lose the war. That day I won the fight, but ultimately lost the best friend I had all because I allowed a few instigating idiots and a few Iron Mike Tyson titles go to my head. I didn't want to fight, and Tommy boldly said he didn't want to fight either before he ever threw a punch. So why did we fight? It was because if you don't tell people who you are, they will decide who you are for you. The power of attorney was in effect.

Since my first fight, the spectators decided to call me Iron Mike, which intrigued me to research, study, and train to be like him as well. But what I soon learned is the fact that there is only one Iron Mike, and more importantly there is only one Koran Bolden. It would have been ok to emulate the hard work ethic and dedication that Mike Tyson possessed, but at the end of the day I can never be like Mike, nor did I want to be him. By ditching my identity as Koran Bolden, I took on the identity of someone else and that's where most people fall into the greatest danger of life.

This experience in life has been so engrained in my mind that I still remember it like it was yesterday. The good news is that our failures often lead us to success if we learn the lessons from our mistakes. Who would have known that a small fight on a playground in New Orleans at the age of 6 would be a crash course entrepreneur lesson on how I would later deal with irate and dissatisfied customers in my own business.

To be successful we must develop a high tolerance level for dealing with people and their diverse personalities. Some personalities that people possess can be a direct conflict against your personality which can cause high levels of friction and disagreements. But through it all, if you blow up or cause a scene, even if you were right, you lose because nobody wants to do business with an angry person. When facing emotional challenges, here are some take aways I learned that will help you cope with disagreement and conflict. My conflict resolution tips are as follows.

## Body Language

**1)** In the midst of a heated discussion or disagreement, always respond with a calm voice. I am a motivational speaker and so my passionate voice carries heavy weight when I speak. My hands move when I talk, and my eyes light up like Christmas trees. Although I don't mean any harm, a person from a different background or upbringing can take my simple hand gestures and heavy bass filled voice as a threat. Be mindful of how your body language is truly being perceived by the other person you're communicating with and you will master the art of communication.

## Genetics

**2)** Jail cells all across the world are filled with people who wish they could have changed the hands of time and walked away from a conflict. All it takes is being at the wrong place at the wrong time with the wrong attitude, and the reputation that you worked so hard to build is gone in seconds. If you seem to feel like you have a low tolerance for dealing with ignorance, it's ok. You must understand that we all have been born with a genetic coding that drives and gauges our personality and our tolerance level. Some people are born genetically wired with higher tolerance levels for conflict and some can blow up quick at the pettiest things. My best advice is to understand who you are and try to surround yourself around the appropriate people and environment that fits your personality style. In cases where there are clashes in personalities, find ways to cope from the irritation and take some communication classes ASAP. Business men and women with low tolerance levels for conflict need to make sure they are highly equipped in the area of communication skills. Head rolls, finger pointing, and disgruntled faces can speak louder than your words and will not be tolerated in the marketplace.

## Cultural Differences

**3)** It has been said that people on the East coast are some of the most obnoxious and direct people you will ever meet. For the most part they are very blunt with their opinions and sometimes can be brutally honest with you even if it hurts you feelings. They can have a heated discussion with you at the point of almost getting into a fist fight and moments later after they calm down can have a cup of coffee with you as if the argument never occurred. But some people won't take your direct communication style the same way in business. You may have been raised in a household where it's a norm for people to be yelling and screaming, but that doesn't mean it's the norm for the person you're communicating with who grew up in a household of gentleness. Learn to understand and express your views in the way of the person you are talking to if you really want to be a master of being heard and get your point across.

## Follow Your Heart

**4)** Follow your inner voice at all cost, even if it means walking away and coming back later.

## Word Selection

**5)** When you're in an escalated argument, both parties are no longer listening to resolve the problem. It is now a mudslinging match to see who can hurt the other person the most. Never speak while you're frustrated. You may say something you deeply regret later. You can always apologize but you can't take those words back. Always remember a soft answer can calm even a furious man.

---

## The Fence

I read an interesting story. There once was a little boy who had a bad temper. His father gave him a bag of nails and told him that every time he lost his temper, he must hammer a nail into the fence. The first day the boy had driven 37 nails into the fence. Over the next few weeks as he learned to control his anger, the number of nails hammered daily, gradually dwindled down. He discovered it was easier to hold his temper than to drive those nails into the fence.

Finally the day came when the boy didn't lose his temper at all. He told his father about it and the father suggested that the boy now pull out one nail for each day that he was able to hold his temper. The days passed and the young boy was finally able to tell his father that all the nails were gone.

The father took his son by the hand and led him to the fence. He said, "You have done well, my son, but look at the holes in the fence. The fence will never be the same. When you say things in anger, they leave a scar just like this one." You can put a knife in a man and draw it out. It won't matter how many times you say I'm sorry, the wound is still there. Make sure you control your temper the next time you are tempted to say something you will regret later.

 **Rock**- I went up against my core belief system for complete loyalty to friends.

 **Paper**- I didn't have a list of personal rules to define my friendship. One of those rules would have stated to never fight my friends.

 **Scissors**- Although I heard my friend clearly state that he didn't want to fight, I refused to become courageous and let the outside voices control me.

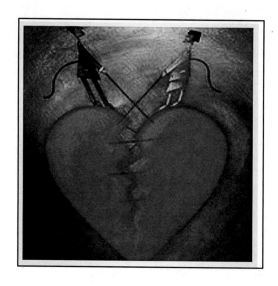

# CHAPTER 4
# THE POWER OF MANAGING YOUR EMOTIONS

"For every minute you remain angry, you give up sixty seconds of peace of mind." -Ralph Waldo Emerson

## The Emotional Scale

Understanding and embracing your emotional gauges can be one of the most beautiful things about our human biological makeup. Your emotions are strong currents of energy that can transfer from person to person. This energy can make a bad situation good, or a good situation bad. If this is true, why do so many people think communication is so complicated and run from expressing how they truly feel? Here is the answer. We fear what we don't understand and can't control. But here is the truth. You do have the ability to both understand and *control* your emotions. In Jack Canfield's effortless success program, I came across a diagram that changed my perspective on emotions. Emotions are vibrations mixed with our thoughts to make things manifest. The higher or lower you are on this list leads to the quicker your thoughts manifest. Good or Bad. Please view the diagram below.

## Maximum Positive Energy

Level 10: Joy, Appreciation, Empowerment, Freedom, Love, Passion

Level 9: Enthusiasm, Eagerness, Happiness

Level 8: Positive Expectation, Belief, Optimism

Level 7: Hopefulness, Contentment

Level 6: Boredom, Pessimism

Level 5: Frustration, Irritation, Impatience, Feeling Overwhelmed

Level 4: Disappointment, Doubt

Level 3: Worry, Blame, Discouragement

Level 2: Anger, Revenge, Hatred, Jealousy

Level 1: Insecurity, Guilt, Unworthiness, Fear, Grief, Depression, Despair, Powerlessness

## Maximum Negative Energy

"When it all boils down to it, emotions were never created to be destroyed, they were created to be transferred." -Koran Bolden

## Maximum Negative Energy Explained

Our emotions can be viewed as strong vibrations that get us to act on what we are thinking. Don't believe me? Be honest! Have you ever been so angry with someone that you felt an uncontrollable urge to physically or verbally abuse them? That's because you're at the second highest level of Maximum negative energy. In grade school, I use to be so upset that my father was never around that I would blow up in rage and do things I'm surely not proud of today. Now at the moment of these outbursts of anger, I would say whatever rolled off my tongue and I didn't care whose feelings I hurt in the process. But after I cooled off and came back to reality with my true self, I would soon become fully aware of what I had done and would feel extremely guilty. I was full of guilt, depression and unworthiness.

Once the smoke clears you find that you have now entered level one which is the lowest level. The guilt sets in your mind because once you said something you can't take it back and you acted outside your true character. This is an extremely bad place to be. If you are at this level, don't be ashamed to talk to a friend or seek medical or spiritual assistance. This level can be turned around and it won't take as long as you think if you have the right people coaching you one day at a time to get back on the right path. To sum this all up, if you have emotional challenges and difficulties, it's ok. It could be in your DNA passed down through genes, or it could be that you have had some traumatic past issues that happened in your life to cause it. In either case, as long as you feel some conviction when you do wrong, things can be turned around. If you don't feel any conviction when you do wrong please seek some medical assistance. There is help available.

## Maximum Positive Energy Explained

Maximum positive energy is like a flowing river of life. This is the level where most people strive to be everyday of their life. Yet, most never experience it because they choose not to fully understand their emotions. They don't want outside circumstances to constantly control them. It is extremely important for you to wake up and be on level 10 everyday. If you don't intentionally get on this level, there is a huge black hole vacuum that is waiting to suck you down as soon as you step out of bed.

Whenever I'm on level 10 I am fully accepting that something great is about to happen to me. I often confirm this feeling by saying words like "Something good is about to happen to me. I can feel it." And sure enough, every area in my life starts to change. My finances, my faith, my family and my business improves; new ideas flow, and the right people come to help me fulfill those ideas.

Here are a few examples that happened to me when I made a conscious intentional decision to get on level 10. When I'm on this level, I don't seek success, success seeks me.

## Quick Success Stories

*Opened up the mail and received a check for almost $3000 2 months before it was expected

*3 complete strangers walked into my business and gave me a collective donation for a total of $500. They all stated that a force unknown to them was pulling them to give the money and they didn't know why. They had no idea I was dead broke and had a hard time paying my business rent.

*The County Executive's Office heard about my wife and I partnering with Gap Inc., and decided to surprise me in a local Banana Republic store with a proclamation that declared March 21, 2014 as Koran Bolden Day in Saint Louis County.

*Banana Republic heard about my humanitarian efforts from a thank you letter that I wrote them. They then decided to give my wife and I a shopping spree and an all expense paid trip to Las Vegas to deliver a speech on stage at their conference. They stated that this was the first time in history that they had ever decided to fly in a customer to speak on stage. They had received millions of letters from across the world, but out of the blue they picked my thank you note like a needle in a haystack! Coincidence maybe? I think not.

---

## Level 10

These are just a few short stories of what happens when you consciously and intentionally get on level 10 everyday. Once again, it will take a lot of determination and work to stay on this level and some days you will fail miserably. However if you stay the course, you will notice a deep sense of peace and effortless success that opens great opportunities even though you may not be more qualified than others that desire that same opportunity. When dark days come knocking at your doorstep, just refuse to accept negativity as your reality. Just shift gears and intentionally get on level 10!

## He Said, She Said

---

"Great minds discuss ideas. Average minds discuss events. Small minds discuss people." -Eleanor Roosevelt

---

I have noticed something that causes great conflict and issues and this is people who are always speaking negative and gossiping. Gossip surely has the ability to destroy the closest of friends if you let it in. As a person trying to achieve greatness, you must deal with gossip as if it is a hammer and nail like the previous story. Gossip will destroy your dreams every time it's spoken or listened to. Read this story below as a great example of how a wise man dealt with gossip.

## Testing for gossip

In ancient Greece, Socrates was reputed to hold knowledge in high esteem. It is recorded that one day an acquaintance met the great philosopher and said, "Do you know what I just heard about your friend?"

"Hold on a minute," Socrates replied. "Before telling me anything I'd like you to pass a little test. It's called the Triple Filter Test."

"Triple filter?"

"That's right", Socrates continued. "Before you talk to me about my friend, it might be a good idea to take a moment and filter what you're going to say. That's why I call it the triple filter test. The first filter is Truth. Have you made absolutely sure that what you are about to tell me is true?"

"No, "the man said, "Actually I just heard about it and ..."

"All right," said Socrates. "So you don't really know if it's true or not. Now let's try the second filter, the filter of Goodness. Is what you are about to tell me about my friend something good?"

"No, on the contrary."

"So", Socrates continued, "you want to tell me something bad about him, but you're not certain it's true. You may still pass the test though, because there's one filter left: the filter of Usefulness. Is what you want to tell me about my friend going to be useful to me?"

"No, not really."

"Well," concluded Socrates, "if what you want to tell me is neither true nor good nor even useful, why tell it to me at all?"

---

## The Solution To Being Angry

Simply stated, anger is negative energy that has found its way into your body. It can come in through something you saw, heard, felt, or experienced in life. Here is the solution. Find a way to release negative energy and positive energy out of you daily through extracurricular activities such as reading, journaling, poetry, songwriting, sports, and exercising. You can also calm your emotions by helping others. If you don't find a way to release negative energy, I can assure you that you're going to blow up at the wrong place at the wrong time. It's a lose lose situation for all parties involved.

---

"The best revenge is massive success." -Frank Sinatra

---

## Becoming A Power House

When you don't release and share the good inside you, then you will start to feel insignificant and without a purpose. I daily fill up on positive energy and release it the same day as well, so that no negative energy has a way to come in. I do this through praying, meditating, reading positive stories, conversing with positive people, working towards my goals, and helping people reach theirs. Find ways to stay positive and you will be more likely to attract positive people and situations in your life. It's called the law of attraction!

---

## Summary

The reason I have chose to start early in the chapters with anger and conflict resolution is because anger cannot be exemplified if you want to be a man or woman of high respect in business. Your ability to keep your cool in all situations is the foundation of your success. You cannot be a person who responds to external situations with internal frustrations.

Dealing with different people from different backgrounds can be very challenging and can tempt you to act according to your feelings. Every time you allow anger to overtake you, then you become a demolition manager to your own dream project. It can take months, years, or even decades to build a brand, but one act of anger can knock it down overnight. Choose today to take full control over your emotions by walking by faith and not by sight daily. Over time you will have full control over your emotions. If you fail in your attempt to control your temper moving forward, it's ok. Be man or woman enough to apologize for your mistakes and move forward quickly. It's not you blowing up that makes you a loser, it's how you feel and handle the situation afterwards that makes you one. Choose to be the bigger person. It's not about who's right and who's wrong, it's about righting your wrongs. That's more important.

## Meditation Exercise

Recall the last big argument or disagreement you had with a colleague, family member, mom, dad, co-worker, husband, wife, etc.. Now take a moment and identify and jot down why you were upset. Be specific in the emotions you felt during the disagreement.

_____

_____

_____

_____

_____

_____

_____

_____

_____

_____

_____

_____

_____

_____

_____

_____

_____

_____

_____

_____

Now, ask yourself. Have I fully released all the negative energy and moved forward by forgiving this person?

Yes/No

If your answer is no, I would now like for you to close your eyes, take 3 deep breaths inhaling positive energy and exhaling the release of all negative energy. Make sure you are in a comfortable and relaxed position. Now instead of harboring the feelings and emotions that were associated with the conflict, I would now like for you to reenact the situation that occurred in your mind, but imagine being the peacemaker, and being the leader of the conversation by steering things to end on a good note. Replay this situation over and over with you being fully calm in your voice tones, facial expressions, and body language. End the story with you walking away in full peace, then open your eyes.

Now that you have experienced what this solution could have been like, recall this meditation exercise the next time conflict tries to come your way. Stay calm and polite and steer the conversation into a happy ending and watch how well your next disagreement goes. You will take charge!

# CHAPTER 5
# DEALING WITH LOSS

"The darker the night, the brighter the stars,
The deeper the grief, the closer is God!"

After living in New Orleans, Louisiana for a little over 2 years, my mom decided to move back to Saint Louis so we could be closer to our family again. This was a great opportunity for me to have a great influence from some great male role models in my life. It was important to me since my dad was never around in my life to show me how a man is supposed to act. I had an awesome brother, sister, mom, uncles, aunties, and grandparents who were such a loving support system for me. My grandmother was deeply implanted in her faith in Christianity. My grandfather worked at General Motors all his life and was said to have never missed one day of work in 40 years. My sister later in life became the valedictorian of her class at Soldan High, and my brother was a recent graduate from Ranken for heating and cooling. This is the model I had set before me to follow: a family who worked their way from 7 kids being raised under one roof, to a good middle class working family.

My brother Anthony was the one who I especially looked up to. He was my hero in so many ways. He dedicated a lot of time pouring brotherly love in me so I started to look at him as a father figure. I looked up to him so much that I didn't even care that my father was barely around. What made him really spectacular to me was that he had just bought a brand new cherry red Kawasaki motor cycle which was a really big deal at the time considering where we were from. I can still vividly remember him coming to pick me up and letting me ride the back of his motor cycle. Heads would turn on every street we drove down while onlookers were continuously giving us two thumbs up for being super cool. I loved my brother so much that I would literally be in tears when he dropped me off at home.

## The Night That Changed My Life

One day I was abruptly awakened out of my sleep and for some strange reason I decided to go into the living room. It was late at night and so I wasn't expecting anyone to be awake except for me and my pet parakeet bird named BJ. But to my surprise, I wasn't the only person awake. I heard several people having a conversation at the front door downstairs and I decided to be curious and take a peek.

At the bottom of the steps was my mother talking with my two aunties. Although I couldn't quite hear what was being said, I heard my auntie say to my mom, "He's gone." She then embraced my mom with a huge hug of comfort. I missed most of the conversation but knew something fatal had just happened. I left from overlooking the upstairs living room banister and swiftly ran back and put my head under the cover and went back to sleep. My mind couldn't really comprehend what was happening, but something deep down in my soul felt like a piece of me had just died.

The next morning I awoke and things were different. My mom kept crying but didn't want to reveal anything to me yet. Then at my grandmother's house, she pulled me in the kitchen and wanted to break to me the bad news. She said, "Koran, I have something important to tell you," with tears still flowing down her face. "What is it mom?" I asked in a small silent whisper. "Your brother Anthony has passed away." My face overflowed with tears of deep grief and sorrow that no experience of my life has yet to match yet. It grieved me even more to find out that a gang member decided to gun down my brother because of his recent success as a college graduate. He couldn't accept the fact that my brother had just bought a brand new motorcycle, so his jealousy overtook him and he decided to gun down my brother right around the corner from my grandmother's house.

The next few days I was truly in disbelief and still couldn't believe my hero was gone. The man that could do no wrong in my eyes, that had superman like qualities was now taken away from me because somebody couldn't control their anger and jealousy. It just wasn't fair. At my brother's funeral, the visions of seeing him laying in a casket sent a devastating blow and dose of depression to my body that finally resonated with the fact that my brother was gone forever. That's the day that my life changed, and this is also why I am big on showing people how to deal with their anger.

---

## My New Mission

Have you ever lost someone or something dear to you that upset you to the core of your soul before? Maybe it was losing a loved one or maybe it was something that had sentimental or materialistic value to it that you extremely held high in value. The pain you endured after the lost is truly unexplainable and the tormenting thoughts of reasoning says, "Why do bad things happen to good people". After all my years of dealing with the loss of my brother and losing other things that have been dear to me, I have found that the world may never find the answer to this mind baffling question. But there is life than can come from death if you allow it to. The story of me losing my brother has been a great inspiration to others to see me move forward in spite of the fact that this horrific incident happened to me. It is a fact that good and bad things happen to us all, but the difference maker between those who stay down and those who decide to rebound and get back up is located in our response after tragedy occurs.

## Understanding Grief

Dr. Cross, is a highly respected psychologist. I have had the pleasure to work with him on several city initiatives that try to prevent youth violence before it starts. He once said something profound at a meeting. He said that most people that experience being family or friends of a victim of violence, hurt far worse than they are supposed to because they don't know how to properly grieve and cope. He said that when you lose something dear to you, it is vital that you take an adequate amount of time to deal with the severe trauma.

Most people try to keep themselves busy so they can ignore dealing with the grief or stay down for too long, but at the end the whole family suffers. My family sure did. I tried to ignore the passing of my brother and tried to be strong and ended up harboring feelings deep inside me that should have been properly released. Instead of dealing with the issue first hand, I went from an A and B honor role student to a C, D, and F student that did just enough to get by. Although I was intellectually smart enough, and capable enough to outperform and outsmart most kids in my classroom, not going through the grieving process kept those negative emotions resting inside me. It created a worse cycle of like energy to overflow within me.

I became an antagonizing disruptive class clown whose reputation was tarnished to a point of no return after countless fights, suspensions, and trouble that would soon follow me. I just wanted to be alone. I was shut off. When I tried to do right, I would fail time and time again. I gave up because the slightest act would end in me going to the principal's office. Due to my large reputation of disruption, my teachers developed a low tolerance level for having me anywhere close to their classroom.

I was deemed and regarded as a failure. My behavior was so bad that at one point a doctor once told my mom that I would probably end up in jail. Little did they know that they are not the ones who could determine my past, and they surely aren't the ones who have the power to determine my future. My emotional failure was due to the fact that I lost something dear to me and nobody ever thought enough about me to understand that my acts of disruption were actually a cry for help from the grief I was enduring at such an early age.

I was not as bad as they thought. I was just a frustrated kid who got dealt what seemed to be an unfair hand in life and didn't have a proper outlet to grieve and let that negative energy out. How blinded our society is that it only looks at the tip of the iceberg versus seeing that an out-lash or disruption from our youth is really a deep cry for help. It's a cry of a person who has been desiring to do right, but nobody will have enough patience and compassion to steer them in the right direction.

## Don't Be So Judgmental

If you know anybody in your life that seems unhappy, think first before you're so quick to judge. That person could be crying out for help, and if all you do is idly watch, judge them, or ignore the situation without investing love seeds in their life, you are just as much of the problem as you are the solution.

---

"Do not let any unwholesome talk come out of your mouths, but only what is helpful for building others up according to their needs, that it may benefit those who listen." -Ephesians 4:29

---

## My New Found Passion For Music

As time moved forward, so was my calling to do something big. I was going through some old boxes of 12" vinyl and some old dirty cassette tapes one hot summer day and found something unusual. Some of the tapes had my brothers named scribbled on them, so I decided to pop in the cassette and take a listen. To my surprise, I heard my brother on the cassette tapes acting as if he were a DJ on a radio station. I burst into laughter as these were the only memories I had of him since he had passed away other than a few pictures.

At that moment, I felt like I was finally happy again. I felt a bolt of energy shoot through my body to follow in his footsteps and I accepted a new love and appreciation for music. I immediately pulled out a sheet of notebook paper and began to write anything that came to mind over a few instrumental rap songs. Shortly after, I began to get notoriety from rapping in the school yard and at local talent shows. I was soon joined by my best friend Robert Jackson and we recruited several others to join us in forming a rap group of 4 called the Top Dawgs! Years later, the group grew apart and Rob and I continued moving forward.

I remember Rob and I wanted to get a record deal so badly that we would catch the bi-state bus to work after school and spend our whole paycheck on studio time. One year I calculated the amount of money we spent on studio time and discovered we had invested over $10,000 and we were still in high school. Wow! We had no clue how much money we had spent but when you have a dream time flies, and so does your money as you invest. My mom also invested a hefty amount of money, even though she stated several times that she hated rap music. But she vowed to herself that she would do anything that she could to keep me off the streets so that she wouldn't lose another son. It seems as if her hard work has paid off years later and so I respect all the single mothers, fathers and parents who have lost a child and are doing all they can to support their kids talents to keep their kids off the streets or out of jail.

Like my wife now says, "I will support my kids financially in whatever their hearts desire. I would rather pay to keep them out of trouble, than to later pay to get them out of trouble."

### Your Hard Work Will Pay Off

Later, our hard work paid off. We later got some major respect and heavy radio play in our city, which led to the interest and live audition of one of the greatest hip hop record labels of all time called Def Jam Records located in New York. This was the new beginning of stardom for us!

## CHAPTER 6
## MULTI MILLION DOLLAR RECORD DEAL

"When I stand before God at the end of my life, I would hope that I would not have a single bit of talent left and could say, I used everything you gave me." -Erma Bombeck

### A Day and Life at Def Jam

It was 10 a.m. as I sat in a taxi headed to audition for the infamous Def Jam record label – about to ink a $150,000 recording contract at the age of 20 if I played my cards right. Never in my life had I been so excited and nervous at the same time. Everything I had hoped and wished for all came down to one single moment.

If I succeeded, I would finally reap the benefits of all my hard work and labor to become a famous musician and make my mom proud. I had visualized it all in my head – the money, cars, clothes, big houses … What would I buy first? Better yet, this would be the moment that I'd finally say "I told you so" to every teacher, principal and counselor who ever doubted me in school growing up.

On the other hand, this could also be the moment of epic failure, a thing that seemed to follow me often on other projects I'd tried and failed at numerous times before. But somehow that gave me even more determination to win. I truly believed with all my heart that I would be the next Jay Z or Kanye West, and would finally impact the world with my talent and gifts just as I had always dreamed.

After paying the cab fare, I stared up at what seemed to be a mile-high building that no picture or TV show could quite capture as an image of New York City. My heart was pounding and I could hardly believe that I was about to meet *the* Kevin Liles, President of Def Jam – a legend and pioneer in music who started as an intern at the multi million-dollar Def Jam Empire with Russell Simmons. I checked in, escorts came to get us, and the doors opened. It was lights, camera, action – do or die time. Everything I'd worked for since the age of 12 would be determined by one five-minute audition with no second chance. Liles walked into the room, sat down and said, "Let me see what you've got."

With tons of butterflies in my stomach as I sat and waited on Mr. Liles to get off his conference call, I was thinking in my head, "Why in the world am I so nervous?" I had been imagining this moment all my life. I had been practicing and performing for thousands of people before I got here, and there was only one of him. Now that I'm older and more mature, I have learned that butterflies are a good thing. It doesn't mean you're afraid. It means you take pride in your work and you want to do your best.

This was the moment. He got off the phone and said "Let me see what you've got." He pressed PLAY, and we immediately snapped into my zone. Courage rose up, all my fears left us and we performed like we had never performed before – full of passion, determination and energy that said we refused to be average, because we never thought of ourselves as average.

After the performance, Liles paused as I and the other two members of my group impatiently waited. He called some other people into the office for a second opinion. I remember thinking, "Huh? Do it all over again? We just performed a perfect show, there is no way we can repeat it!" We had practiced all our life, but nobody ever asked us to perform twice. Little did I know that practice doesn't just make perfect, practice makes permanent. Once again, the courage rose up and we performed again even better than the first time. Liles stopped the music in the middle of the performance and abruptly said, "I've heard enough." With a grin on his face, he politely said, "Welcome to Def Jam!" We all jumped up and down in the office with joy. A $150,000 record deal that would turn into a multi-million dollar deal was now ours.

---

"People who say it cannot be done should not interrupt those who are doing it." - George Bernard Shaw

---

# CHAPTER 7
# WIPE OUT

"Pride goes before destruction, a haughty spirit before a fall."
Proverbs 16:18

## The Wrong Outlook And Attitudes

It was a cold winter day, and tons of invite only family and friends began to quickly fill a local Saint Louis night club. The attendance turnout had become successful despite of the snow storm that just hit, but we were ready and determined to finish the last day of our video shoot as planned. Finally I got a small introduction to experience what true stardom felt like. In one corner you could see 2 or 3 makeup artists working on the faces of the models in the video, in another you could see the proud faces of family and friends staring in awe at the huge lights and 10-man camera crew. "I can't believe I finally made it," I thought to myself.

## Quiet On The Set

Quiet on the set! Quiet on the set! The video director yelled from the top of his voice. We are going live in 5-4-3-2-1 action!

Finally the moment had arrived that I was finally living my dream. No more practicing, grinding, and working hard to achieve a national recording contract. That time was finally here. Anybody who has ever achieved a goal in life that's working hard knows the feeling I'm speaking of. It's the same feeling you have when you learn to ride your first bike on your own after numerous bruised arms and scraped knees from losing your balance. The same feeling that overflows a young high school or college graduate after walking across the stage from vigorous years of hard work and studying through the wee hours of the morning. The same feeling as a mother feels after holding her new born child after 9 long months of labor or how a man and woman feel after their big wedding day. It's an out of body experience that cannot be explained in words, but if you have experienced any of the like, that's what I felt at that moment.

## It's A Wrap

"Alright everybody, it's a wrap. It's time to go home," were the final words I would hear that day. The conversations and congrats would finally come to an end and the achievement of getting the deal was now over. The hardest part had now come which was to maintain the record deal through more hard work. This was the new challenge ahead that we would face. Sudden fear rushed my mind that night on the way home. What if we fail, what if we lose, what if our group doesn't agree on major decisions? Then the bigger question came to my mind. What are we going to do to make this group a big success? After all, I only walked, talked, spoke and believed I would get a record contract. I never thought of what I would do "AFTER" I got the record deal. I wished we would have had some "Paper" to write it all down on.

## The Awful Break Up

Not even 7 days later our group began to hit a down pike. Ego's started to flair amongst us as it often does with any highly young, talented, and influential rap group with an out-of- the blue promise to become famous. . We had prepared all our life practicing for the big stage, but we failed when it came to creating a unified team vision. This is why having a collective vision is a necessity when it comes to building a brand. The vision needs to be plain and simple so that when disagreements take place, the deciding judge is the mission statement.

The mission statement always reminds all parties involved *why* you're doing what you're doing. In most cases, having a mission statement can put out the most fiery organizational conflicts, but since we decided that our talent was sufficient enough for success and ignored having one we were doomed from the start.

Our social and emotional flaws soon came to the forefront after buying new town homes, cars, jewelry, and clothes. This is exactly the direct opposite of what Mr. Kevin Liles expected of us. He told us to stay focused and to stay humble as he had seen his fair share of the most talented artists fail through inflated egos before. I guess we must have been so excited that we chose to have selective hearing that day because we were on the road from success to failure and fast.

## Oh No, Not Again!

While traveling all over the country, being seen on national television stations such as BET and MTV, my rap group was finally headed somewhere, and fast. But we soon learned that it's much harder to maintain success than it is to gain it. Things started getting rough especially in my mind. I kept having this weird feeling like everything was going to be taken from me, and it was.

I would annoyingly call my manager Donald every hour on the hour asking him did he hear anything new from Def Jam about the next steps to our record deal. He would always reply, "Not yet." Then one day the phone rang. It was my label executive Dave Sherbow calling to deliver the bad news that Mr. Kevin Liles had resigned and we had lost our record deal. I couldn't believe it. But that's not all, things began to turn for the worse.

Bill collectors had started calling and harassing me and my family left and right. The fear forced me to pawn $10,000 worth of jewelry to make partial payments on delinquent bills. However, with no residual income coming in, after a few months I forfeited those items and lost everything. I can remember like yesterday, after months of hiding my car at my mom's house from the repo man, it was finally time to surrender. It was finally time to let go of all the materialistic items and thinking that held me bound. It was time to face the grim reality that I was only prepared for a record deal from a talent sense and wasn't truly mentally ready and prepared from a leadership business sense for my big day.

Fame, fortune, money, cars, clothes, beautiful town home, all gone in a flash. And the worst part about fame was that nobody knew I had lost it all which only reminded me of my failure. I continued to get praises from people when I stepped out the house. "Congrats Mr. Bolden. We heard about your record deal with Def Jam. We sure are proud of you." With a little pride left all I could say was thank you while deep down inside I knew my life had hit a rock bottom dead end.

What was even more horrific was that the people I had stepped on with my hot air balloon ego on the way to the top were now the same people I had to see on the way back down. In a matter of months, I was completely broke. My dream had come and gone in the blink of an eye. I wish I would have had my Rock, Paper, and my Scissors handy.

### Summary

"Far better to live your own life perfectly than to live another's perfectly." -Bhavard Gita

### What is Success?
Success is defined as the accomplishment of an aim or purpose. The only issue is that as humans we have been so brainwashed into believing that the way one person reaches success has to be the same way that you have to reach success. The truth of the matter is that most people who have reached success got there by ways that weren't imagined, planned, or controlled.

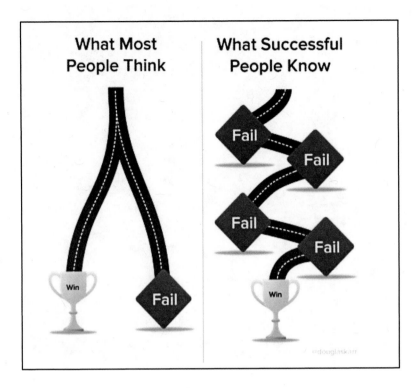

In the case of this record deal, I thought that the only way to become wealthy, famous, and valued was to hopefully meet some DJ's that play my record on the radio to get discovered by a major label. But boy was I wrong. Destiny was calling me to something much **bigger** through a road less traveled. I was being called out to be different and to use this story to inspire hope in a hopeless world. As you will read later, success truly has multi-facets of unique paths for us all to follow, but if we try to follow behind someone else's' path in the exact same way they achieved success, we will surely get lost on the journey specifically designed for us.

# CHAPTER 8
# THE YOUNG PROFESSIONAL

"Success is walking from failure to failure with no loss of enthusiasm." -Winston Churchill

After losing my record deal with Def Jam, things began to get hard for me. There was so much going through my head at the time and to top things off my girlfriend LaPortcia informed me that she was pregnant with my first child. At the time, I made a conscious decision to take care of him and be there for him so that he could have the life I always wanted. Although an opportunity presented itself to me to go to Atlanta and chase my music dreams again, I chose to man up and stay in Saint Louis to take care of my son.

This decision was made after hearing the replay in my mind year after year of my mom always telling me to make sure I remember what it feels like to not have my father around, and to make sure I use it to fuel me to break the cycle. That replayed in my head over and over and was powerful enough to lead me to make the decision stay behind and watch as from afar as the other two members in my group went on to Atlanta to continue pursuing their dreams. My time of pursuing my dreams to be a rap star was officially over in my mind.

## Climbing the Ladder of Success

One thing you will soon learn if you haven't already is that entrepreneurs have to embrace having periods of loneliness. This rough moment in life comes because we don't always have the most popular ideas about life. We normally go up against what the world is doing to fit in, Instead, by refusing to conform, we stand out.

There were many days I cried myself to sleep with the hurt, pain and regret from all the people that I stepped on to get to the top. That haunted me for a long time. I then learned a valuable lesson about fame and fortune that most people don't have the courage to confess. Materialistic produced Fame is an addictive drug that can lead to great danger if not controlled. Every person that you step on going up the ladder will be the same people you will have to see when you come back down the ladder and that hurts more than you ever can imagine.

I can assure you that we all will come down one day, but if you have treated people good on the way up, those under you will give you a helping hand when you slip on the ladder to the success and will help push you back up. But this was not so in my situation. Everybody left me and surprisingly nobody ever called to check and see how I was doing. It was as if I was wiped off the face of the earth. But LaPortcia had birthed an amazing son which gave me a new hope to live on and strive for excellence.

## The First Day Of Work

For starters, I mentioned that I wanted my son to have everything I didn't, so the fact that I was in his life was 90% of the battle for me. But I wanted him to have it all by me being the example. So I decided to face the cold hard thoughts of a man that lost a record deal going back to work for minimum wage. What an experience on my first day of work. I had to start somewhere because I didn't have much of a job history because I had been doing music all my life.

The first day at work was really weird for me. Walking to my seat hoping I didn't think anybody would notice me.... But... I was wrong. Some of my colleagues knew exactly who I was. In fact, my video was still playing on some television stations and the embarrassment of the questions that followed surely hit me hard. "What in the world are you doing working here if you're supposed to be so famous," they asked. All I could do was hold my head up high and know that my new mission statement for being a great father was the reason I was there. I was there for one reason and one reason only, and that was for my son to see his dad leaving and going to work every day to put food on the table. That's all that mattered.

I immediately became so focused that I quickly became the manager and supervisor of projects, and main go-to guy for everything from training to strategy. I went from $7 an hour, to $8, to $9, to $10 and so on until I built up my resume to get a better job in corporate America. By learning from the results of what happens to people without a plan and strong work ethic, I decided to develop a strong dedication for advancement and I ended up landing a job with a temp agency that got me my job at Brown Shoe Company.

## Brown Shoe Company

After filling out tons of applications and going to countless job interviews, my hard work and persistence had finally paid off. I got my big break when a local temp service staffing agency found me a position at a Fortune 500 Company. The position I was hired for would allow me the opportunity to move from the bottom to the top of the organization with plenty of room for company promotion and advancement from the world renowned Brown Shoe Company. Just FYI, Brown Shoe Company is the leading shoe company in the world who designs, manufactures, and sales the top shoe brands in the world such as Carlos Santana, Dr. Scholl's, Famous Footwear and Shoes.com just to name a few. This was another chance for me to use my talents and gifts to work my way up the corporate ladder and become a company asset and influencer. Dreaming big with another temp that started with me named Lekardo, we both dreamed big that one day we would become the CEO of the company as we both enthusiastically gave our best everyday to accomplish this goal that we spoke.

I clocked in early, stayed late, worked overtime, and committed my all to get where I was going, and fast. Then a problem approached me that would once again challenge the greatness inside me. My supervisor Donna, had been listening to some of my phone calls in which I received several bad scores on. What made me so frustrated was that when she wasn't monitoring me, I gave the best customer service ever that often followed by numerous customer compliments and emails to my supervisor. However when she sat next to me, I had become extremely nervous. As soon as I would see Mrs. Donna come my way, the palms of my hands would start sweating profusely, and my heart would literally beat through my chest from all the adrenaline that would flow through my entire body.

On my last monitoring, Mrs. Donna warned me, as she plugged into my headset, that this would be my final chance to keep my job. If I did well, I would be hired full time, but if not, I would need to clear off my desktop and drawers and leave the premises. Yikes, so much pressure! All my other co-workers that started with me had got hired including Lekardo, but for some strange reason I felt as if it was lights out for me at this point.

### So What Do You Think Was The Outcome?

Well, the call came through the phone and to no surprise, just as I thought, I received the WORST customer attitude ever. With my hands sweating and heart pounding at maximum speed, I began to become discombobulated with my words, thoughts, and computer screen menus. I had been on the sales floor for weeks but I was fumbling around like I had never been trained at all. Without warning, Mrs. Donna politely unplugged her headset jack and walked away in the middle of the call. I already knew the outcome. Shortly after the call, Ms. Donna called me to her office and informed me to contact my temp agency so they could deliver a message to me. When I called my temp agency they told me to turn in my ID badge and leave the premises immediately.

My corporate dreams of becoming CEO was over and another failed attempt had found its way to my mental doorstep. "I knew it, I can't seem to do anything right. I always get the short end of the stick," I thought to myself internally.

**It's Not Over, Until You Think That It's Over!**

---

"If You're Tired Of Starting Over, Then Stop Giving Up."
-Author Unknown

---

Right after receiving the devastating phone call of my termination, I sat at my desk with half of my items put away in my bag and it hit me. "I have come way too far and have worked way too hard to let my future go down the drain this easily," I shouted with a voice of triumph in my mind. I came from a family of winners that never raised me to be average or mediocre in anything, and I have had enough of my past thoughts bullying me. It was finally time to take charge of my life and put this life tormenting bully on a boat back sailing to where it came from.

I put my stuff back on my desk and asked Ms. Donna for a meeting. I sat down calmly and looked her in her eyes and told her that I really wanted my job and how there was no better candidate for this position at Brown Shoe Company than me. With a blank stare at me, Ms. Donna replied, "You know what Koran, I don't know why I am about to say this but I'm going to give you another chance." It's amazing how diligence and desire mixed with the faith to act can change you from a failure to receiving another chance. She told me to study my systems and company manuals over the next few days as she was going to give me one last try in a few days. So I went home, *got focused*, and did just that. I got lost in the moment.

## My Last Shot

---

"Everything you've ever wanted is on the other side of fear."
-George Addair

---

The next day, everybody in the office heard I had a final chance to prove myself and tried to encourage me to be calm and do my best. But while I appreciated their support, their encouragement really didn't matter at this point. I was dealing with something much bigger than a job on my hand. I was now facing a habit of limiting beliefs that was trying to kill me as a person. This bully was about to take food off my family's plate. It was now time for me to step in the ring, and have the fight of my life which was to regain control back over my life.

A few weeks later, as promised, Ms. Donna came to my desk to monitor my next few calls. I tried to have a little small talk with her while we waited on the next call to buzz in, but Ms. Donna didn't want to have any conversation of the sort. She was on a mission to look out for the best interest of the company. Surprisingly, the calls were slow that day, which made it a little uncomfortable as we waited for incoming calls, but I kept thinking the best. In my head I thought the best and believed in myself. "Come on Koran, you got this in the bag. You overcame the loss of a record deal. You overcame the loss of your brother. You overcame not having your father in your life. Nothing on this earth can stop you." No matter if the next incoming call was a customer complaint or not, I had decided in my mind that they were going to get the best customer service the call center had ever received that day. Then a beep came though, and I answered. It was show time. "Thank you for calling Brown Shoe Company, this is Koran Bolden, how can I assist you today?

Needless to say, I received several happy customers back to back and I passed the monitoring evaluations with flying colors. This secured my seat at the best company I have ever worked for in my life, Brown Shoe Company!

## Ms. Donna Resigns

The next day I decided to come into work with a hand written hallmark card of appreciation for Ms. Donna for giving me another opportunity to redeem myself. When people do great things for you, I suggest you do the same if you plan to stand out and be extraordinary. As I approached her desk, I noticed she was doing some packing of her own. As I handed her the card and began to thank her, she abruptly stopped me in mid sentence, packed the rest of her items from her desk and asked me to help take her cart to the garage. As we walked to the garage, Ms. Donna told me she had decided to resign from her position at Brown Shoe to accept a new offer from another great company. I was in awe. She told me as she left, that she was amazingly surprised that my passion moved me to approach her for my job even after she told my tempt agency I was terminated. Donna was known as having a get it done-no-play no-games type reputation. But due to the fact that I courageously fought for my job, touched her to have a change of heart. As we loaded her items in the car, she reaffirmed how much she believed in me. She told me that I had a special gift filled with passion, and as long as I stay true to self, I would go a long way in life. To my account, nobody other than close family members had ever told me they genuinely believed in me so much, since the lost of my record deal. With my spirit uplifted and my head now raised higher than ever, I gave Ms. Donna a final hug and farewell and the beginning of my life as a young professional had begun. I had finally defeated the Goliath size giant called failure that had tried to intimidate me and was now ready to dream the impossible.

---

## Summary

I am no different than you. In fact I have learned the greater the pain, the greater the gain. After countless hours of interviewing and studying millionaires, and billionaires, they think and use these same principles. So my question is today, what issues and adversities are you currently facing? Losing your home, with no where to stay? Car just broke down? Risk of getting kicked out of school? Losing a scholarship? Lost a job and can't find work? Relationship or marriage on the rocks? Well, I'm here to remind and encourage you. My faith moved mountains at Brown Shoe Company that day, and so can yours! You are extraordinary. It's time to fight back!

---

"You have a choice. You can throw in the towel, or you can use it to wipe the sweat off of your face." -Gatorade

---

 **Rock-** I believed that this job was mine even though my current circumstance said otherwise.

 **Paper-** After a second opportunity was given to me to redeem my mess ups, I went home and studied the proper information needed to succeed.

 **Scissors-** I got extremely focused. When I came home from work, I immediately spent the rest of my off time studying. No TV, no hanging out with my friends. I had to sacrifice to win.

# CHAPTER 9
# I Have A Dream

"If you set your goals ridiculously high and it's a failure, you will fail above everyone else's success." -James Cameron

After going through the ordeal with Ms. Donna and getting hired as I previously informed you, I was moving up the corporate ladder. I began to help my department in major ways. I was always willing to work extra overtime. I got promoted to assistant training supervisor and even won employee of the month. I was on a roll at this point. That CEO position began to slowly drift back in the inner part of my mind once again. Then another pivotal moment happened in my life. A true game changer.

## Street Dreamz Gives Birth In My Mind

I was sitting in my living room one evening, living out the normal daily routine, and suddenly was blasted with a thought that I was not supposed to be a CEO of Brown Shoe Company but a CEO of my own company called Street Dreamz Recording Studio. I paused for a second in awe, asking myself what in the world is Street Dreamz? The voice was so distinct and powerful that it made me jump off the couch and immediately grab a pen as I began to write down a ton of ideas and thoughts that followed. The next moment, I wrote out a full business plan that included a mission statement, budget, and target audience that I would reach. Before I knew it, I had a few pages of jotted notes in my hands with emphasis in bold, scribbled circling around a $15,000 startup budget. That's when reality kicked in. To be honest with you, I didn't have anything to put towards the $15,000 investment. In all honesty, I had bad credit. I had no mentors, no degrees in business, and was living check to check with bills that swallowed my check even before I got paid. But for some strange reason my mind wouldn't let me stop thinking about this brand new recording studio that would call me back to the music industry where I once failed miserably.  So to push past all my fears, I did the best thing I knew to do. I called a few friends and told them all about this new business startup idea.

After telling a few people of my new business venture idea, to my surprise I found that most people weren't as excited as I thought they would be. I received mediocre excitement from mediocre people. On my last phone call, I put the phone down and my soul cried deeply. I was truly disappointed that my big vision didn't receive big approval but instead the warrior of greatness rose up on the inside of me and said, "Speak out and repeat out loud that which I have spoken to you." So from that moment forward, through faith, I spoke 1000 words everyday as soon as I woke up about this brand new leadership studio called Street Dreamz. I didn't have a mentor, but that was ok. I soon learned there was an organization in every city that has tons of the best mentors and thought leaders of the world called the library. I got my first ever library card and I studied, and I spoke. I studied and I spoke. I even drew out a mock floor plan on a napkin even though I didn't have a building yet. By the end of my planning, I decided that I would have the first leadership recording studio located in a mall, and nothing would stop me from completing this task.

The most interesting thing of all is that right when this idea was presented to my mind, it was right at the beginning of the bank bailout and house market crash of 2009. The news was loaded daily with discouraging news about tales of the greatest economic failure since the great depression was approaching us. This led to people withdrawing their money from banks. Nobody wanted to spend their money on recreation, so why would they want to book recording studio sessions? The world was in an economic uproar that sent a message to the public to hold on tight to their money because businesses were filing bankrupt left and right.

Now you can probably only imagine what I was thinking in my mind. If big multi-million dollar corporations are filing bankrupt and in threat of losing it all, what would this mean for a new kid on the block like me who hasn't even started. But those reports didn't move me. I was a man on a mission to achieve the unachievable, to break the unbreakable, to stand out and shine when there was nothing but cloudy skies all around me.

To make matters worse, rumors began to spread at the office as well. With the news reports of recession rising, many corporations were forced to restructure the way they did business. Some of my coworkers began to confront me about my idea to start a recording studio. After listening to all the views of why it wouldn't work, my inner voice of greatness began to fade and I had to make a decision by myself.

Should I quit and give up? After all, I don't have any money.

Technology has been the death of the recording industry. Will anybody still want to record at my studio?

Maybe I should play it safe and hold off on the new business venture for a while because times are about to be hard. Besides, what if they lay us off like the news says?

## Dealing With Uncertainty

---

"Too many of us are not living our dreams because we are living our fears." -Les Brown

---

Then it was time to make a decision. It was now time to sink or swim. There comes a point in life when you're going to have to quit dreaming and put your faith and dreams into action. So what did I do?  LaPortcia Although I was totally discouraged and confused about  my vision, I made up in my mind that the next morning I was going to push myself outside my *comfort zone* and take my faith to the next level by spending my whole check to buy a brand new iMac computer from the Guitar Center. This computer cost about $900 and this was a big step for me because I only got paid every 2 weeks and my bi-weekly check was barely that much. But I didn't care. I was determined to make it happen. I had made my decision and had officially become known that day as a real entrepreneur. One who takes a higher amount of risks than others, to achieve higher levels of success than others. That day, I risked losing it all by buying a brand new iMac computer so that I could live the life of an award winning entrepreneur!

## Honey, I'm Home!

I remember looking at LaPortcia, who back then was just my girlfriend and the mother of my son. As I came in the house and unpackaged the beautiful slim screen computer on the table, she then gave me a strong look of deep confusion that I had never seen her do before. Now LaPortcia was one of those good people who had always believed in me. She listened and watched me develop countless other ideas. She witnessed these ideas go down the drain and still supported me no matter what. But this one was a little far left field because the world was in an uproar from the economical slumps from the stock market crash. The idea of starting a recording studio was good but, "Why in the world would you start it now," she wondered. The reason I did it was because my vision was bigger than me. I wanted to open a recording studio to be financially stable and to use my talent and gifts to help other students live their dreams. I also wanted to have an opportunity to work with industry music professionals that I didn't have the chance to work with when I was growing up.

Needless to say, I kept on speaking 1000 words everyday and the most amazing thing about it is that I made it the next

2 weeks with food on my table, gas in my car, and clean clothes on my body without any money. You'd be amazed at how creative you can get when ramen noodles are your only option for dinner. It was tough, but we sacrificed and made it through. Although this was the best move I ever made in my life, at the time I didn't know what I was getting myself into. But thank God I moved forward.

## The Big Lay Off!

Then one day I came into work, and all my coworkers were completely quiet. The atmosphere was extremely dark and I knew something had happened. As I walked onto the sales floor a few of my co-workers said, "Did you hear about the layoff?" I replied,"Huh? Layoff?" I knew if they were going to lay anybody off, with the luck I had in the past, I would surely be the first to go. I then opened my email as instructed for more information, and it read:

Dear Mr. Bolden we are undergoing a lay off and you fit in that group to be released.

My head fell down low and I immediately began to pack my table.

But what was to follow totally revolutionized the reason I now believe in the power of the words we speak and what can happen when you begin to believe. One of my co-workers interrupted my pity party and tapped me on the shoulder. As I turned around, they looked at me with a grin of joy and said, "Read a little bit lower at the bottom of your email." I hadn't even thought to read the rest. I was being laid off! All I could think about was what I was going to do to put food on the table for my family.

## As I scrolled down the email it read:

Mr. Bolden, although this lay off we are undergoing will be a great concern for most, we have decided to send you away in the best situation possible as you look for your next position with a severance package according to how long you have been employed. And then it said the amount I was to receive. Can you guess how much it said?

If you said $15,000, you guessed right. The exact same amount I had written down on the notepad had found its way to force my job to lay me off with the exact amount I needed to open my new business. With my head held high, the most influential recording studio called Street Dreamz was now born. This should be a true testimony that the words we speak are powerful. They are more powerful than we can ever imagine.

---

"Consider it pure joy, my brothers and sisters, whenever you face trials of many kinds, because you know that the testing of your faith produces perseverance. Let perseverance finish its work so that you may be mature and complete, not lacking anything. If any of you lacks wisdom, you should ask God, who gives generously to all without finding fault, and it will be given to you. But when you ask, you must believe and not doubt, because the one who doubts is like a wave of the sea, blown and tossed by the wind. That person should not expect to receive anything from the Lord. Such a person is double-minded and unstable in all they do."
James 2:8

---

 **Rock-** I believed, in spite of how much bad news was being reported on the news about the failing economy.

 **Paper-** I wrote down a business plan on a napkin and viewed it daily. It included a small floor plan and an estimated budget. Nothing extravagant or intense detail.

 **Scissors-** After making the big mistake of asking mediocre minds what they thought of my recording studio idea, I cut off all those outside voices by taking my full paycheck to go buy my first studio computer and it all paid off.

# brilliant |ˈbrilyənt|

adjective

**2** exceptionally clever or talented : *a brilliant young mathematician | a brilliant idea.*

• outstanding; impressive : *his brilliant career at Harvard.*

• Brit., informal very good, excellent, or marvelous : *we had a brilliant time | [as exclam. ] "Brilliant!" he declared excitedly as she finished telling him what had happened.*

## CHAPTER 10
## BE YOUR OWN BOSS

"If you don't build your dream,
someone will hire you to help build theirs." -Tony Gaskins

### Becoming Your Own Boss

Now on to the exciting stuff you've all been waiting on! It's finally time to discuss how to develop an award winning brand from scratch. No more scratching your head on how to bring your dreams into fruition. Here is my simple guide on how to take those extraordinary concepts that are in your head, then mold them into physical Mona Lisa like masterpieces.

## Let's Get Started

Now that we have discussed how to properly develop building your faith, disciplining your disappointments, and building the capacity for a solid character, you are now in a great position to build a *reputable* brand.

The reason I chose to deal with this subject in the latter part of the book is because you can't build a strong foundation without your values being defined and perfected. Most upcoming young professionals and entrepreneurs are so passionate in faith that they lose rational thinking. They have the ability to build a beautiful bridge, but don't have the proper mentoring to bolt down the bridge to have a strong foundation. In the end they become discouraged and extremely exhausted from all their hard work and labor and have nothing to show for it. They build a bridge and watch it burn because their personality and unsteady character diminishes their trust in people. Eventually, they end up burning their bridges. When it comes to building a brand, trust is everything. When you're selling people the concepts to your dream, you are actually asking them to cross over to your way of thinking on a bridge you created, and if they don't see your bridge as a credible source via verbal and non verbal cues, they will never buy in to traveling on the journey with you.

Consequently, if you decide to skip any of the baby steps of developing a solid foundation of character for your company to stand on, the success you achieve will literally crush you, and I do mean in a literal sense. You will start out strong but finish weak like I did when I pursued a major record deal. In the world of business, this is not a race for sprinters but is more like running a marathon. Ask anybody who has ever ran a long distance race what happens if you rush through the proper stretching, preparation, and training before a marathon, and they will tell you that the end will be worst than before you began. It would have been better for you to not have started at all.

---

"There will come a time in your life where you will eventually have to stop playing double dutch with your dreams. You have been planning and waiting too long. Don't let the fear of getting hit by the rope stop you from jumping in the game." -Koran Bolden

---

## Turn Your Passion Into A Paycheck

With today's technology, anybody can go online and become an established business owner in their state with a name and debit card in a matter of 45 minutes. However, building a brand takes strategy, patience, perseverance and intentional execution at the right place and time if you want to last. The days are long gone of people buying into the hype of another self proclaimed entrepreneur being introduced as the CEO of XYZ Incorporated as their title on a business card. To truly be respected, it's going to take more than a business card to become the king of the hill in your industry. You're going to back up your gift of gab with some substance.

## Finding Your Purpose

One of the hardest steps to becoming an entrepreneur or leader in your field is taking the first step. Day in and day out people are clocking in and out of their job unfulfilled, unhappy, under appreciated, and underpaid. This indeed is a major problem with our world right now. We have the wrong people in the wrong positions which stunts the growth for global innovation. Let's face it, if you're not happy at work, the people around you know it, and after a while you spread that negative cancerous energy into the entire workforce. Why don't you do us all a favor! Quit bringing your negative cloud in the workplace and do something that truly makes you happy!

"Success? I don't know what that word means. I'm happy. But success, that goes back to what in somebody's eyes success means. For me, success is inner peace. That's a good day for me."
-Denzel Washington

## Happiness Hygiene

Just the very thought of leaving your job or moving to a new challenging position in your organization is scaring the crap out of most of you reading this book right now, and it should. If you don't feel some form of fear when you step outside your comfort zone, I would be reluctant to ask if you really stepped outside your comfort zone. To sum it all up, to be happy in a world filled with negativity all around us is a challenge. But remember our crash course in the earlier chapters. Negativity can be around, but it's your choice if you decide to let it in you. You are the captain of your ship. Being happy is a full time job that must be managed, nurtured, and cultivated and there is no such thing as being happy by doing something your weren't called to do.

One of my youth leaders Kevo Yancey, pinned the tail on the donkey when he said, "There is no amount of practice that you can do to make you be great at something that you were never created to be." Don't let a paycheck run your life. Do what you love to do, whether an intrapreneur or entrepreneur. Your passion alone can generate a greater paycheck that you can ever imagine when you are experiencing maximum happiness. This is how to move your way to the top without playing office politics and competing with everyone in the marketplace. When you focus on your passion, your work will be so great that it will speak for itself. This is the first foundational block for building an award winning brand. When you're unhappy and depressed with your work, that's your body giving you cues that you are not doing what you were created to do.

**People who are in the wrong workplace or own the wrong business normally show the symptoms below**

* You come in late, and leave early

* You're constantly looking at your watch to see what time it is before your next break or time to go home

* When a customer comes in your store you don't greet them politely. You ignore them as if they don't exist. Hoping that they don't ask you for help because you want them to leave the store.

* When your boss asks you to go above and beyond, you catch an attitude and think to yourself, "This wasn't in my job description when they hired me. They don't pay me enough to ask for such a task from me."

* Massive gossiping and complaining

* When you first started your new job you liked it, then after a few months or so once you got settled, you completely hate it

### People who are in the right workplace or own the right business normally show the symptoms below

* You come in early, and leave late

* You're so passionate about what you're doing you often lose track of time

* You're impatiently waiting on the next customer to come in the door because you get a chance to sharpen your communication skills and satisfy a new customer with your product or service.

* You expectantly look for ways to grow your organization. You are proactively searching and brainstorming on new ways to make the customer experience more efficient and effective.

---

Whether you work for yourself or you're working for others, these are the things that will indicate if you're in the right position or organization. Don't waste your life. Either apply for a new position, or go looking for a place where you can utilize all of your God-given gifts and talents.

### What If I Don't Succeed When I Leave?

"It's much greater to fail at something big than to succeed at something that's irrelevant." -Arnold Donald
CEO of Carnival Cruise Line

While I am a firm believer that all things are possible, I also must be brutally honest with you about achieving great success in today's business world. Being an entrepreneur has been one of the hardest tasks I have every faced in my life. From the first day I wrote my business plan on paper, to the day I opened my doors, I have grown physically, spiritually, emotionally, and mentally in ways I cannot explain in words. I have experienced desperate times where if a customer didn't immediately walk through my doors, I would literally lose everything I had. There were times when my wife LaPortcia and I would wake up and realize that we had no gas in the car, and would have to do a scavenger hunt for loose change in the couch and under the bed just to get to work. But through all the fame and success and television interviews people never knew about the sacrifice we had to endure to become successful.

I know what it feels like when you are running around town trying to get people to believe in your vision and it seems as if nobody is listening. I know what it feels like to have everybody less qualified around you supersede you in success, and you can't understand why you haven't caught your big break. I know what it feels like to have people try to hop on your moving boat but then jump ship when the storms come. There is a quote from one of my favorite books that comes to mind when your calling to be great becomes so overwhelming that you feel like throwing in the towel that says this. "The race is not given to the swift, nor to the strong... but for those that endure to the end."

"Average people get average results if any at all." -Arnold Donald
CEO of Carnival Cruise Line

Arnold Donald said it best at a leadership program I attended. He said, "Sometimes you won't succeed at everything despite your greatest amount of effort." That statement completely shocked me. Why? Arnold Donald is one of the most successful African American men in the world. To hear him share his story about moving up the ranks in the world from being poor to being wealthy, one would assume that everything he put his hands to would turn to gold. His transparency from making this statement swept the room with complete awe to the point that you could hear a pin drop. Some of us relaxed with sighs of relief as his truth on the misconceptions of obtaining true success was being debunked.

As much as our celebrities make achieving success look effortless, there is much more to achieving greatness than the eye can see. In life there will be times when you're extremely confident to the point where you're willing to jump off the ship and walk on water, while in other circumstances you will jump off and start sinking and will need others to pull you out of the raging waters back to safety.

Yes, you will continually make mistakes. Yes, there will be times you feel deep regret as if you made the wrong choice, but at the end of the day I would rather come to the end of my life saying I gave it my all versus saying, "I could have. I should have. I would have." Don't be afraid to reach beyond your limits. I'm not saying quit your day job tomorrow, success happens with opportunity meets preparation. The question is are you preparing yourself to jump ship when the time presents itself.

## The Right Timing

Right before I got my $15,000 severance package from Brown Shoe Company, I was on the verge of quitting and starting my own business. If I would have quit, I would have left at the wrong time and missed out on the answers to my prayers. The one simple act of obedience to stick it through and be patient enough to wait and prepare for the right time opened up the doors for me to live my dreams. Arnold Donald finished this unforgettable speech by saying, "There is no effort without error and short comings." Don't be afraid of what may happen if you don't step out the boat, but instead ask yourself what all will you gain when you do step out.

## The $400,000 Office Depot Contract

It had been a week of hard work and my mind and body was completely exhausted. I had been running errands all day long to the point that I just wanted to go home and get into bed. On my way home I noticed a small car on the side of the highway with its hazard lights on which appeared to have several small children in the back seat. Now normally I always get out and help, but this time I was just too tired. As I passed their car and saw the desperate and frustrated faces as I drove by in my rear view mirror, I felt my heart drop. I thought to myself, "Koran, it will be ok. You always get out and help people. They will be ok. Just like you noticed them, someone else will notice them and come to their safety. Go home and get yourself some rest." The only problem is that my compassion was overpowering me and those thoughts went straight out the window. My intuition

88

was telling me to help them because they were in possible danger.

Then I started to wrestle with my thoughts for a few more seconds because at this point it would take me 15 minutes to circle back around to meet them. "What if somebody comes to help them before I get there? Not only will I have wasted my time, I would have wasted my gas too," I thought to myself. Finally, without further debate, I turned my car around. It took me 15 minutes to come back around to them. As I parked and approached the stranded vehicle, I noticed 3 little beautiful girls all under the age of 10 sitting in the back seat. In the front seat, was a young couple in their mid 20's with a sign of amazement on their faces. They couldn't believe I came to their rescue. I then walked up to the driver's side and asked the young man if he was ok. He then replied, "Yes." He began to inform me that his family stayed up the street and they were on their way to pick him up and get the car off the side of the road.

Now anybody that knows me will tell you that I strongly believe that everything happens for a reason. I knew that my intuition didn't tell me to turn back around for no reason. Then it hit me. I looked the young man in his face, and told him how much I believed in him. I told him that the calling on his life was great and how he was called to change his generation. I then shook his hand, gave him my business card and walked away. About an hour later I received a phone call from an unidentified number. As I answered, the young man began to joyfully thank me. He then told me how he knew God had me turn around to go check on him. He said that nobody had ever looked him in his face and told him that he had a purpose in life like I did and he would never forget me. He told me that my words just changed his life.

## What Goes Around, Comes Around

About 1 hour later I received another unidentified phone call, but as I answered there was a different person on the line. It was a guy by the name of Tom who I met a year ago who mysteriously found my business card and decided to reach out to me to potentially partner on a big project that came his way. On the first phone call, he stated that there was a huge nonprofit foundation that wanted him to interview and audition for a big upcoming national school tour and he wanted to know if he could use my name in his presentation as a potential tag along. I replied," Sure, why not." We hung up from the call and I thought nothing else of it.

Later on that day, I received another phone call. It was Tom again. What he said next blew my mind away. He said, "Hey Koran, I googled your name online and saw all the amazing things you're doing in your city. The foundation that I am going to audition for said that I can bring my partner with me and I would like to extend the invitation to you." I was amazed. I met Tom a year ago and I would have never expected him to call me because when we met we only talked for 15 minutes at the max. Now out of the blue he calls and extends an invitation to me on an all expense paid trip to Boca Raton, Florida at an internationally acclaimed foundation? Wow!

Believe what you want, but good deeds given freely surely know how to come back around and repay you. I knew that my random act of kindness with the young man in the stranded car had landed me the opportunity to travel with him. My name was put in his heart to partner with me because what goes around comes around. When you do good things for other, others will do good things for you.

To make a long story short, the foundation that wanted us to audition for this speaking tour was the Office Depot Foundation. They had solidified a partnership with the super group One Direction to bring awareness to bullying and wanted to put together a 300 school tour across the country for a whopping $400,000.

When Tom and I arrived in Boca Raton, I couldn't believe my eyes. Our hotel rooms were beautiful. On my bed sat a letter from the Office Depot Foundation informing us to enjoy our stay with special made cookies with the Office Depot logo on them. I felt like I was dreaming, but this was no dream at all. In less than 12 hours I would have the opportunity to solidify the contract of a lifetime.

---

## The Big Audition

The next day Tom and I pulled up to their facility and sat down with the CEO of their foundation and presented. We were asked question after question on how we would be able to adapt to speaking nonstop on this nationally promoted tour. We gave our assurance that we were the best men for the job and they informed us that they would be contacting us soon.

On the flight back home, I looked out the window in amazement. I continually thought of how solidifying a contract at this magnitude could empower my family and career as a speaker. My spirit reminded me of just how important it is to continuously do the right thing in a world where it's so easy to get distracted to doing the wrong thing. After I returned home, I impatiently waited for the phone call of the good news that we were selected to head the tour. I couldn't wait to jump for joy and tell my family the tour start date.

Three weeks later, Tom received a phone call from the agent over the project. The agent broke the bad news that we were not picked to head this awesome tour. They had selected someone else for the job.

Ouch! Once again, so close to success I could taste it and I was denied access. The next few days were hard for me, especially coming home breaking the bad news to my wife and kids. In my opinion, we were the most qualified for the position but we came up short. While bad news like this would totally devastate some from ever trying again, I was able to live in total peace knowing that I had put my best foot forward. To be honest, if I had to audition all over again, I wouldn't have changed a thing. I was able to recover from disappointment and move forward understanding that if this opportunity passed me by after I gave my best, that means that there is something better for me out there. And although it surely didn't feel like it, since Office Depot is such a big organization, I had to trust and believe that something is happening behind the scenes in my favor that I couldn't physically see.

To say the least, my audition on an all expense paid trip that I had no idea was a possibility showed me that possibilities are endless when you believe. To all those who are afraid and worried in life about which direction you should turn in life, this story is for you. Be hopeful. Be of a good cheer. Know that all things will work together for the good. Not only did I leave with an amazing experience, I also understand that if this happened for me once, it can happen for me again. God surely knows how to make a way out of no way.

## Summary

"There is only one way to avoid criticism: do nothing, say nothing, and be nothing." -Aristotle

My simple suggestion for those that feel like it's time to go to a higher level is to ask yourself to define what true happiness looks like on paper. After you take the time to put your passion on paper, it's now time to ask yourself if what you are working on now is moving you towards your passion or away from it. If the organization you are working for is investing in you as a leader, giving you opportunities to build your resume and put some experience under your belt, you may want to stay put. On the other hand, if you feel like coming to work is a burden and you hate your job, I'm sorry to be the bearer of bad news but you might want to embark on a new journey. Life is way too short to spend your life in an unhappy place. Your bad attitude is going to show in your work and get you fired in the long run so you might as well start looking to do work that you're passionate about. Some jobs and positions are seasonal.

## How Do You Know When You're Operating In Your True Calling?

When I am working on building a new product or platform that I am passionate about, I get lost in the moment. I literally lose track of time and my hard labor to get work done no longer feels like work. It feels more like a hobby. When I am in this passion zone, I'm happy, I'm productive, I'm creative, I'm stress free, I'm worry free, I am vibrant, I am successful. This is how you truly know you are doing what you are called to do. It has nothing to do with the amount of money I'm making but has more to do with operating in my area of giftedness. When you are in your calling you don't mind facing the daily challenges that come your way. Most Millennials say that they are willing to take a pay cut to do what they love to do versus making a lot of money but not impacting the community! From this moment I dare you to be brave enough to step out of your fear zone and to step into the clear zone. When it comes to living your dreams and a life full of no regrets, there is nothing that compares to it. The grass is truly greener on the other side!

## CHAPTER 11
## WHAT IS A BRAND?

"You cannot build a reputation on what you're going to do, you can only build a reputation on what you've done." -Henry Ford

In simple terms, your brand is a company's reputation and personal promise. This guarantee is often associated with a person or symbolic logo that then creates and summarizes expectations and perceptions of what to experience when they interact with your organization. A brand is often known by its trademarked logo which often represents the total experience. Overtime, the brand becomes so heavily engraved in the consumers mind, that if you say the name or see the logo your senses are already heightened to perceived expectations. When you're building a brand, *consistency* is the main ingredient. If you ever violate the expectations of your brand on any level, you can lose customers quicker than you gained them.

# Why Is Building A Brand Important?

## Joshua Bell's Metro Performance

A man sat at a metro station in Washington DC and started to play the violin; it was a cold January morning. He played six Bach pieces for about 45 minutes. During that time, since it was rush hour, it was calculated that thousands of people went through the station, most of them on their way to work.

Three minutes went by and a middle aged man noticed there was a musician playing. He slowed his pace and stopped for a few seconds and then hurried up to meet his schedule. A minute later, the violinist received his first dollar tip: a woman threw the money in the till and without stopping continued to walk. A few minutes later, someone leaned against the wall to listen to him, but the man looked at his watch and started to walk again. Clearly he was late for work.

The one who paid the most attention was a 3 year old boy. His mother tagged him along, hurrying but the kid stopped to look at the violinist. Finally the mother pushed hard and the child continued to walk turning his head all the time. This action was repeated by several other children. All the parents, without exception, forced them to move on.

In the 45 minutes the musician played, only 6 people stopped and stayed for a while. About 20 gave him money but continued to walk their normal pace. He collected $32. When he finished playing and silence took over, no one noticed it. No one applauded, nor was there any recognition.

No one knew this but the violinist was Joshua Bell, one of the best musicians in the world. He played one of the most intricate pieces ever written with a violin worth 3.5 million dollars.

Two days before his playing in the subway, Joshua Bell sold out at a theater in Boston and the seats average $100.

---

This real life story of Joshua Bell sums up the reason you need to be very intentional about building a brand. This story above is a perfect example of how you can have the most amazing talent in the world, but if you haven't built a brand, your talent may never get a second look because the world is just too busy. A brand gives you a platform. When you stand on a platform, your voice elevates over everyone else and puts the spotlight on what you have to say. No brand, no voice.

## We All Have A Brand

Building a brand is important because whether you like it or not you are currently building a brand. For example, let's say you were asked to attend a party and you see two women sitting in opposite corners alone. One woman was thought of as being drop dead gorgeous wearing a tailored high end designer dress while the other was viewed as the everyday average Joe Smoe dressed very conservatively with reading glasses. Although both of these women are off in a corner and to themselves and haven't said a word all night, they both are exuding a brand that is being perceived by everybody in the room without their consent whether they like it or not.

The woman who is dressed in the fine clothes and silent may be viewed by others in the room as:

*Snobby                    *Bougie

*Proud                     *Conceited

*Uppity                    *Snooty

*Stuck-Up                  *Arrogant

The woman dressed very conservatively and silent may be viewed by the others in the room as:

*Shy                       *Bashful

*Gentle                    *Quiet

*Soft-Spoken               *Submissive

*Timid                     *Low Ranking


Let me remind you that neither one of these ladies have said one single word all night but they're already being sized up, judged, and **branded** even though these assumptions could be completely false. The point I'm trying to make here is that we all have a brand whether we like it or not. The clothes we wear, our associations, our viewpoint, our tone of voice, our facial expressions, our values, our opinions are all making a statement verbally and non verbally which is creating a brand (expectation or reputation) constantly. Knowing this, if you want to be the top in your field, respected, valued, and heard you're going to have to become very intentional about developing your brand corporately and personally. Otherwise, you could be sending mixed signals that can make it harder for you to break through this over competitive marketplace.

## A Brand Gives You A Valued Voice

"It's Not What You Say, or How You Say It,
It's All About Who Says It!" -Koran Bolden

Let me start by saying that a brand can only be as powerful as the person who owns it! A successful brand speaks volumes so you don't have to. Don't believe me? Have you ever been in a conversation with someone who argues back and forth with you even when your advice is 100% right, and it seems as if you're talking to a brick wall? Nothing seems to get through to them. Then afterward, a complete stranger comes along who has higher credibility than you, who gives the same advice you gave word for word and that person who you argued with receives the advice as if this was their first time hearing it. Totally frustrating right? I know! Well here is why.

There was once an old saying that goes, "It's not what you say, but how you say it". While I somewhat agree with this statement when it comes to timing and voice tonality, I would like to add something that makes this statement even more powerful. It's not what you say, it's not how you say it, but it's more so about who says it. Still don't believe me?

Turn on Dr. Phil and watch how people on his show fall into a trance-like state when he gives his studio audience and the guest on his show advice. Some of the things he says seem to come across a little harsh at times but his credibility overshadows how he says it. Their heads start nodding continually as he speaks in total agreement that he must be right because he is *the world renowned* "Dr. Phil". He has a higher platform that makes him a credible source. It's amazing how credibility can amplify even the softest whispers.

Need another example? Have you ever been to your doctor's office and he diagnoses you based on his expertise from your described symptoms. He comes in the room for 5 minutes, listens to you talk and prescribes you medicine. After he walks out the room most people never ask for a second opinion from another doctor. Why? Because his brand as a doctor says that the man in the white lab coat knows more about health than you do. For all we know he could be as wrong as two left shoes, but the brand of being a doctor is considered a trusted and credible source when we need advice concerning our health.

If you want to have an award winning brand you're going to have to become an expert or credible source in your field. But credibility alone will not do the trick. Credibility may get you in the door, but lack of execution will slam those same doors shut in your face if you're not wise.

When I first started Street Dreamz, I made the big mistake of trying to be modest and behind the scenes not wanting any credit for my work. Instead, I decided to push my leaders to the forefront and build my brand on them. The only problem is that if you build your brand on other people as your spokes persons, if they leave and decide to do something else, the life of your business will take a huge hit. You cannot afford to be behind the scenes with your vision. You need to be on the front line of battle. People may leave, people may become less passionate, but one person that will never give up on the vision is the person who started it.

Below are some words associated with *credibility* to help you have a better understanding of how to build more of it.

### Credible
Capable of persuading people that something will happen or be successful.

*Honorable                   *Respectable
*Admirable                   *Commendable
*Worthy                      *Praiseworthy

# CHAPTER 12
# HOW DO I BUILD A BRAND?

"If you start off trying to reach everybody with your brand, you will never reach that little special somebody. Your brand has to be big enough to speak to the masses, but personalized as if you were having a personal one on one conversation with your targeted demographic." -Koran Bolden

Please listen up! This is the part that is going to save you so much time and money if you listen carefully. The best way to build a brand is to Dream Big, but Start Small.

### Determining the Demographic

The following is highly suggested as a good starting place for those that want to create a brand with extreme clarity. Creating a product or service is always about adding value to the customer. If there is a need, and you have the answer, they will pay you for that answer.

## 1. Create A Consumer Profile (Who)

Create a profile of the average person that would become an advocating die-hard fan of your products and services. Be very specific and thoughtful, then write down what makes them tick.

Male or Female or both?
What's their average age?
Does this person the decision maker or have the power to make the purchase purchasing power? If not, who is?
What do they care about the most?

## 2. How Can You Add Value To Them? (What)

Identify how your product or service will help them save time, money, or headaches. In the world of business and community, your success is determined by how many problems you can solve in the world. The more problems you can solve, the more money you can make. After all isn't solving problems what business is all about? You find a need in the marketplace, and you fill that need with a solution and attach a price tag to the product or service for a monetary exchange.

## 3. When Is the Best Time to Offer? (When)

Identify the peaks and valleys in their buying habits. This will help you know when to market to them. It makes no since to sell Christmas items in the Spring unless you're an overstock liquidation company. Know when your customer needs your help the most.

## 4. What's the best place to sale to them? (Where)

Are they at conferences, in the grocery store, in a shopping mall, or on social media? Find out the best place that they like to buy or socialize. Of course it sounds really fancy to have your own office building which definitely builds credibility, but the main goal is to meet them directly where they are. If you can afford the overhead of having an office building, go for it. If not, look around town and find somebody that may be willing to share an office space with you or let you set up a virtual office. Please don't get caught up in the hype of renting a space if you can avoid it. Your job is to get to your potential clients and meet them. The marketplace is too over-saturated for you to depend on them coming to you. Location is everything, so choose wisely.

## 3. Who Else Is Offering What You Offer? (Spy)

If the supply exceeds the demand, you go out of business. If the demand exceeds the product you become very wealthy. In order to accurately calculate the demand, you must first know who the players on the field are already. No NFL team or any other sportsman steps onto the playing field without knowing the strengths and weaknesses of their opponent. By knowing your competition, you will be able to find ways to better sell what you have to offer.

If you're not going into business to help the world solve problems, you might as well stop right now. It will save you a lot of heartache, pain, and money. The key to both business and community work is all about adding value to others. The more value you add, the more likely you succeed. Point, blank, period.

## 4. Differentiate (Why)

Now that you know the typical person that might be interested in what you have to offer, now it's time to create a consumer profile of yourself. What does this customer need in order to trust you? How can you add credibility to your presentation? Is it your attire? Your packaging? Your customer service? If this was their first time meeting you, why should they be compelled to do business with you?

Before I opened my recording studio, I knew that most studios had theft problems and were hard to find. So what did I do? I decided to open my studio in one of the safest places in America with lots of visibility. The shopping mall provided me with plenty of security, tons of mall traffic every day, and a chance to meet new people and introduce my concept to artists who may not have felt comfortable because of negative stigmas associated with the scandalous music business. About 90 percent of my customer base was from first time musicians that had never been in a studio, and that experience of hearing themselves on a CD for the first time was priceless for them and their family. I ran my business successfully without passing out one flyer because everyone gave me free word of mouth promotion from hearing the buzz about me having a studio in the mall.

## Dominate (How)

Now it's time to drum up some business. Take your brand and spread it over a small town, and then expand from there like a wild fire. At the beginning you will need to do a lot to push the branding ball up the hill, but once you get it rolling, word of mouth with take over and push the ball for you. Go hard with promoting your brand. Don't let up. Don't quit! Motivate your sales team to get out and talk so much about your product with the world that they either hate you or love you. Either way, be so bold that it forces people to pay attention because with so many people marketing to them, if you don't grab their attention you will never get them to buy.

## Summary

Now that you have created a customer organizational profile, you are now ready and prepared to build your mission statement, logo, elevator pitch, and strategy. Starting with these steps first will help you have an amazing start to creating a great business plan for investors and your team.

Remember, if you are so busy trying to reach everybody, you will miss the people who would really benefit from your business. The only way to make your brand feel personalized is to make your messaging feel like you are talking directly to them.

---

"If you're not going into business to help the world solve problems, you might as well stop right now. It will save you a lot of heartache, pain, and money. The key to both business and community work is all about adding value to others. Point, Blank, Period." -Koran Bolden

---

www.StreetDreamzUSA.com

## CHAPTER 13
## STREET DREAMZ GRAND OPENING

"The best way to predict the future is to invent it." -Alan Kay

It was July 3, 2010 and a small crowd started to gather outside a new recording studio that would revolutionize the way people thought about youth and musical empowerment. Finally, the moment I had always dreamed of owning my own business was approaching. I was headed to the mall to make my grand opening speech and the whole ride there I could not believe what was about to happen. After one full year of working hard to make sure everything was perfect before I opened, it felt good for this day to finally come. My heart was beating fast. My chest was pounding. My palms were sweating. My dream was no longer in my mind, it was now in visible form for the general public to see!

Moments before I opened the gate to my store front, I grabbed my wife's hand and held my kids close to me, for they were my inspiration and support group when I started.

I spoke and declared what my business was about to bring forward in the years coming, and tons of people cheered as we prayed over my business together and cut the ribbon. It was a joyous occasion that words cannot explain. I finally did it. I was no longer deemed a failure in my mind as I just made the biggest come back since losing my Def Jam contract. My mom was extremely proud as she smiled from afar as the beginning of something big was now in effect. Street Dreamz was born.

Now I know what you're going to ask me. How can you make the same thing happen for you? Here are a few steps that got me started.

## What's Your Wow?

"At first they'll ask you why you're doing it.
But later they'll ask you how you did it." -Author Unknown

A good friend of mine named Buddy, once came by my studio with his wife. We began to talk about the music industry and he wanted to congratulate me on all my success. Having the mind of a marketing genius, he said that he understood why I was being so successful. He said, "Koran, I respect you because you dared to be different by opening a recording studio in the mall. People need to take a page out of your playbook. You understood that success was not only about mastering the craft, but also mastering the difference in your craft." This is what I was speaking of earlier when I spoke of having the competitive advantage. The fact that our studio was different with its no profanity approach was pure accidental genius-ness. I never knew so many people would be offended that I wouldn't let them record in my studio without using profanity. In fact they were so offended, they told everybody they knew. But little did they know that trying to bad mouth me only sparked more curiosity and stirred up an amazing word of mouth campaign for me which drew even more attention to our brand. My haters gave me free advertisement for my business and I thank them dearly for building a platform of success for me.

Your wow should have the ability to strike a strong emotional connection with your consumers. With so much competition in the marketplace, your brand needs to have such a strong emotional connection with consumers that people either strongly love or hate what you have to offer. There is no such thing as in between. Don't think local, think global. Don't be afraid to take a risk to push the envelope. Here are a few ways build instant credibility.

## Key #1 Start With Your Logo First

Now that you have created a customer profile for who needs your product, it's now time to make things happen. Whenever I am developing a product I always start with the logo first. This is a goal that is fairly cheap to obtain and gives visual life to your project. When a woman is pregnant, the pregnancy doesn't really become official in her mind until she sees her baby's heart beat pumping on the ultrasound, so this is why I start with the logo first. By starting with the logo first you create the heartbeat to your dream. This will significantly boost your confidence to get buy in from others and people will view you as a credible man or woman of business.

## Key #2 Write Your Mission Statement

A mission statement is a must have for any organization to thrive and be taken seriously. A mission statement provides the roots to your organization that prevents you from being moved and uprooted when times get rough. The deeper the roots, the stronger the tree. My mission statement for my studio was to have a non profanity studio that challenged students to find positive and healthy ways to express themselves while getting first-hand experience in the business world. There have been many moments where I was tempted with money to go against those rules, but my mission statement always gave me boundaries to play by and reminded me that money isn't everything. The same people that thought that a leadership recording studio wouldn't work, are the same people asking me for a job now.

## Key #3 Stop Taking Advice From Mr. Mediocre

---

"I owe my success to having listened respectfully to the very best advice, and then going away and doing the exact opposite."
-G. K. Chesterton

---

A business expert by the name of Mike Murdock once said, "Never take advice from a person you aren't willing to trade places with." Mr. Medicare's job is to flood your mind with a bunch of "what if's" and "I tried that before and it didn't work" slogans that discourage you away from your dreams. Part of the reason why they want to discourage you away from your dreams is because somebody discouraged them away from theirs and misery sure does love company.

Stay far away from these people at the beginning of your journey until you're strong enough to handle criticism. Yes, there will be tough times where you will have to listen to constructive criticism as an organization but just getting started is half the battle for you right now. If you spend your time worrying about the things that could go wrong, you will never get started. Only take advice from the experts who have been where you have been, and have gone where you want to go. If all else fails and you still are undecided and you still don't know what to do, always follow your gut instinct.

## Key #4 Start Now. No, Right Now!

"Whenever I hear the words gonna*, finna*, or about to, I know I am having a conversation with a person who never got started on yesterday's task." -Koran Bolden

Starting a business is not a piece of cake. I can assure you that you will spend more time working on your own brand than you have ever spent working on somebody else's job. There will be many tireless nights of research, coffee meetings, and phone calls that will need to be made for you to make your dreams become a reality. Your excitement and enthusiasm will be a determining factor for increased momentum in helping you push this big challenge of owning your own business. The law of diminishing intent says that if you don't get started working within 48 hours of the moment you conceive your big idea, it's unlikely that you will ever follow through to make it happen. It's time for some of you to hit the library or get on the internet ASAP.

## Alexander Bell Invents Telephone

The great Alexander Graham Bell had achieved inventing one of the greatest communication inventions of all time with the creation of the world's first telephone. What most people don't know is that he was credited with this invention by filing the telephone model with the US patent office only two hours before his competitor Elisha Gray. Gray and Bell filed their telephone model drawings on the same day, but Bell decided to send his lawyer to hand deliver his paperwork in person while Gray had been procrastinating for three days to turn his drawing in by mail. Although both men filed on the same day, Alexander Graham Bell was awarded with the credit for the invention of the telephone, but not because he was smarter than Gray. He was awarded the patent because he understood that either you will handle your business, or your business will handle you. Graham's competitive advantage was speed.

Like Alexander Graham Bell's opponent who showed up two hours late, procrastinators and indecisive people have the hardest time breaking through. I know this personally to be true as I am the type that would rather do it the right way the first time than to spend tomorrow cleaning up a mess that I created by rushing through today. But as an entrepreneur, your strategic plan for advancing your organization from good to great is largely based on being aware and prepared as an opportunist as well. Some deals that come past your desk may only be a once in a lifetime deal and you have to be aware when to take off the hat of being the old sluggish and strategic tortoise and become the quick and confident hare.

If you are over analytical, a strategic thinker, major procrastinator, over-perfectionist, or constantly indecisive, it's time for a paradigm shift because entrepreneurs are often opportunists and risk takers. As a word of wisdom for all you perfectionists, don't get so focused on not making the wrong move that you end up making no move at all. Don't go into today's game of life based upon the failures of yesterday. Instead choose to learn from yesterday's mistakes and move forward quickly.

## Key #5 Don't Compromise

One evening a man came walking into Street Dreamz. I immediately greeted him, "Welcome to Street Dreamz, how can I assist you today?" I don't know if this guy was drunk or on some type of ill mannered drug, but the next words that came out of his mouth made me think he was a little on the kooky side. He said, "I know you have that sign up that says no profanity on your wall, but I know that's not the rule for adults. Why don't you let me pay extra and record here using profanity and I promise you nobody will ever know about it," he replied with a wad of fresh 20 dollar bills folded in his hands.

What's so memorable about this moment in my business was that it had been a very slow season in the mall. The money I was making over the summer was not nearly as much money as I had making in this down season which put me in a bad situation for giving in to temptation. By chance, my electric bill to the studio was due the next day and if I didn't pay it they were going to come disconnect service to

114

my storefront which would have served me a full plate of embarrassment to my customers.

Now pondering on what I could possibly do with the money he presented to me, I began to take him on a tour of the studio. I began to review his bribe to overrule my mission statement. After all he was right. Nobody would know but the two of us. I then started to feel sick as he started to put his shopping bags down to prepare to record in my studio vocal booth. "What in the world am I doing? Is this really the tone I want to set for my customers by disrespecting my house of global outreach for money?" I thought to myself. I knew it was time to either record or kindly escort the man out the building and risk the chances of my lights being cut off the next day which could potentially lead to us closing our store for good.

Then it happened! I began to lift that burden of temptation off me by becoming enthusiastic about my vision. I rose up out of my seat and began to recite my mission statement to him with fire and passion. I told him that my business was going to be the greatest entrepreneurial and musical outreach the world has ever seen and we will have locations all over the world to show it. After I went on my three minute rant of bold declarations I asked him to politely leave and record at another studio, even though I knew my lights getting cut off would be a huge embarrassment to the brand. But what happened next shocked me.

The young man began to look at me with pure excitement and stated that he had never seen anybody speak with as much passion as I did. He then stated that he now believed in the vision because he always wanted to do positive music but he never had a cultural outlet that embraced clean music. He then thanked me for my time and left.

Shortly after I began to think about what I had done. I knew I would have to call my wife and tell her that I refused to allow a customer to record because of our mission statement and what was coming our way with the disconnection the next day. But right before I could pick up my phone to dial her number, another customer walked in. Just as with the customer before I asked, "Welcome to Street Dreamz, how may I assist you?" He responded by saying, I want to buy a package for my son to come record at your studio." After I finished going over the package options he then stated that he wanted to get started ASAP and pulled out a wad of money to pay immediately. The package I quoted him was for $2000. Looks like I didn't have to sell out after all. The answer to my problems was waiting right around the corner but if I didn't dismiss the temptation I wouldn't have been available to receive the blessing that was coming my way just 30 minutes later. What an amazing story of faith and integrity.

---

"Things work out best for those who make the best of how things work out." -John Wooden

---

# Summary

In business you're going to have to decide what's best for your organization as a whole, and going up against your mission statement is never a good idea. The lesson that I want you to learn is that before the electric bill problem ever occurred, there was an answer already on the way for my light bill problem. I just had to be patient. If I would have sold out and took the money, I would have felt horrible knowing I missed an opportunity to stand up and be bold and allow my faith to show that we would come out on top. This opportunity will always go down in history for me to stand strong in every challenge no matter what. The problem is not that it's just a one-time act of dishonesty, because you can get back up from that. What the biggest problem with selling out is that after your mind has lowered the standard and you did it once, the temptation to do it again gets stronger to make you a repeat offender. I encourage you to develop a solid mission statement that gives you a reference point for why you started. Then, when times get hard review it for a boost of energy to wow the world.

---

## More Good News

The next few days to follow, the news media began to catch hold of what we were doing and praised our studio because of its mission statement and began to run featured news stories on us. We were invited on the news twice and had the front page of the newspaper all in the same week directly following this fiasco to go against my company policy and values. Dare to be different. What makes you different makes you dangerous to the marketplace!

# CHAPTER 14
# ALL ABOUT THE BENJAMINS

"For the LORD your God will bless you as he has promised, and you will lend to many nations but will borrow from none. You will rule over many nations but none will rule over you."
Deuteronomy 15:6

## The True Intrapreneur

A manager within a company who promotes innovative product development and marketing.

After every speech I deliver on stage, I am always thrilled to see a long line of eager people who were sitting in the audience that have become inspired to follow my calling to be an entrepreneur. Although I am humbled by this, there is something that always disturbs me a little. There seems to always be a group of people who want to do exactly what I do which is to be an entrepreneur, but when I ask them why they want to be an entrepreneur they always give the reason that they are tired of going to work for somebody else. I give a slight smirk but in the inside of my head I'm thinking that if they only knew that starting off being an entrepreneur results in less pay, more work and sacrifice than what's required from their current job. Entrepreneurship is a calling, and so is intrapreneurship. Entrepreneurship is more than making more money, going on lavish dream vacations, and buying foreign vehicles. If you are operating in your areas of giftedness, you can achieve the same results as young professional if you play your cards right. One should never start a business just for the sake of leaving their job to do less work or have their staff do all the work while they are on vacation.

## The True Entrepreneur

---

"A real entrepreneur is somebody who has no safety net underneath them." -Henry Kravis

---

A person who organizes and operates a business or businesses, taking on greater than normal financial risks in order to do so.

For the most part, every entrepreneur that I have personally interviewed has described themselves as the black sheep of the family or a complete weirdo. Yup, you read that right! While people are spending countless hours asking non relevant questions like is the glass half empty or half full, entrepreneurs simply reply, "It depends on whether we just got done eating milk with cookies". We may not be the smartest tool in the tool box or have compelling academic IQ's, but our creativity IQ is often highly admired and described to be nothing less than pure brilliance. The true entrepreneur is a breath of fresh air at any organization as we are the wind that blows the sails of every corporate ship with our innovative thoughts and quick transitions to adapt in any climate change.

I once overheard a conversation where someone said that in order to be an entrepreneur you have to be a risk taker. One who is a compulsive misfit in his/her thinking process while living fearlessly and irresponsibly living on the edge. Well I'm here to serve those crazy uneducated people an eviction notice because entrepreneurs are just the opposite.

We are often analytical-compulsive meaning that we may take a little longer spinning our wheels to get our thoughts into action, but once we make up our minds there is nothing that can make us retreat in the other direction. Our plans are often well thought out and unrealistic to the average mind. Our thoughts can be so far-fetched in the future that it may take months or even years for most people to finally understand us and get on board with our project ideas. We are often misunderstood, non-traditional, highly driven, highly passionate, and often have an out of body experience when we day dream which produces a supernatural confidence, even though our physical minds and self esteem may be uncertain at times.

We are very protective, very intentional, and sometimes introverted, and we also get bored fast with any repetitive operations of work. We will get the process going, but we are too far in the future to stay in the current place in time. We can get the party started but we cannot clean the kitchen when we are done. We have millions of notes in our iPhone, notepads and tablets that we swear could all make us a million dollars or more if we only had the money, staffing and resources to make it come to life. We are often the center of attention and we have the ability to adapt to change quickly.

And finally, while most people say that we are known for taking risk, we think to ourselves that when it comes to doing whatever it takes to fulfill our dreams we aren't taking a risk at all. We believe that living in the world and not living your dreams is the biggest risk anybody could ever take. We are world changes with our unorthodox thinking.

## Don't Quit Your Day Job

"You can't be a good boss to anybody if you have never been a good employee to somebody." -Koran Bolden

A good friend of mine once told me he had the opportunity to meet a Billionaire in a seminar, and to his surprise this billionaire's all time favorite book was the Tortuous and the Hare. When asked why this simple children's story was so profound to him, he simply replied with this. "No matter how many times you read the book, the tortoise always wins".

I have often heard of some people who have talents and gifts and don't know where to start. My response is always this. If you don't have a vision of your own yet, get plugged into somebody else's vision until you do. Life is too short for you to be waiting to get active. Join different groups. Serve at your local church. Volunteer to feed the homeless. As you begin to serve, you start to find what you like and don't like and who knows? You just might come up with your next big idea for success. If it's one thing that I have learned, it's that action begets action so if you ever get in a rut or a creative block, get to moving and watch things begin to happen.

## The Levels Of Success

"You go from cheering in the stands, to playing in the band, to playing on the team, to owning it!" -Koran Bolden

**Cheering in the Stands-** Reaching the first level of success highly depends on your ability to cheer other people on. Supporting others builds your social capital stock quicker than anything else. When you are genuinely cheering others on without expecting anything in return, people will do the same thing for you. If you want a lot of people to show up to your events, make sure you show up at theirs.

**Playing in the Band-** Reaching the second level of success is for those who want to do more than support. Instead of cheering you on from behind the scenes, they actually want to get their hands dirty and have some skin in the game. People who are playing in the band want to be the ones who advocate for you to the point that they cause a momentum. When they serve, their presence alone makes your brand more credible as they hype up the crowd to keep believing in the vision and coming to the games, even when you're losing.

**Playing on the Team**- Reaching for the third level of success is for those who understand the true definition of team work. When you're playing on the team, you go from "me to we" in the sense of a collective impact. You work all year round. You sweat harder. You laugh. You cry. You win. You lose. But ultimately the greatest part of playing on the team is that you have the ability to go down in history by winning the championship. Your eyes are always on the prize for your team to win and make everyone happy who supported you.

**Owning It**- Reaching for the fourth and final stage of success is the pinnacle of greatness. You have successfully experienced all levels of the business and know it's time to own up to maintaining a legacy. On this ownership level, it's more than making money and living a lavish lifestyle. It's about owning a franchise or business that provides the opportunity for others to have a place to gather and believe in one unified vision. For those who reach this level you keep the mission alive and offer job opportunities for people to take care of their kids. This is what it means to live the life of a true social entrepreneur. This is the highest level of success and I pray to God that every person reading this book has the opportunity at some point in your life to own your own future.

---

"What would you attempt to do if you knew you would not fail?"
-Robert Schuller

---

## CHAPTER 15
## STREET DREAMZ GRAND CLOSING
## THE OCTOPUS EFFECT

"I use to think that character was defined as what a man did behind closed doors when nobody is watching, but now I know that true character is developed with what a man does in the midst of controversy when everyone is watching with the doors wide open."
-Koran Bolden

After being featured on the news, my business started to gain some heavy attention. A hip hop recording studio had been open for more than a year now which puzzled many of our doubtful spectators. "How are they still open if they aren't allowing people to use profanity in their music?" they wondered. But time after time I was determined to win. We then started to partner with major corporations and nonprofit organizations which took our reputation through the roof. We had now become known for our youth empowerment service and character education consulting. This led our organization to being sought after to create our own award winning after school programs. We were being booked to speak so much that we were barely at the studio recording anymore. We developed an after school entrepreneurial and music program for parents and students to record at our facility for free by going through the courses. We spoke to over 30,000 students, and we had literally outgrown our leadership capacity. What became a blessing was now heartache because we weren't prepared for the overflow of workload. Our demand had exceeded beyond our capacity to execute and our business began to fall apart.

My workers were at each other's throats when I wasn't there. Gossip and envy grew strong in their conversations and I was too busy to try and fix these issues because I had caught the entrepreneurs disease called the octopus effect.

## The Octopus Effect

The octopus effect is the major reason why nearly nine out of ten new businesses fail. Our gift for creativity mixed with a little ADD causes us to stretch ourselves thin at times. As an entrepreneur, I had to learn that no one is superman and we all have a limited capacity to effectively execute. If we are not careful, we will soon find that we are working up a sweat trying to be productive but soon find out that we have only been running on a treadmill. You can run as hard as you want but at the end of your toil, you have gone absolutely no where. You're in the same position that you were when you finished, that you were when you first started.

So to help every perfectionist reading this chapter, here are a few things that can help you rid the pain of the octopus effect.

## 1. Focus On One Main Target

I once heard a man say that if a genie was to give him three wishes, one of his wishes would be to have unlimited wishes. Although it seems like good thinking, it reveals something deeper in the future failures of his plans. A man that needs more than three when he is told that he only has three wishes is indecisive and has a focus issue.

There should never be more than 3 main points of focus on your desk at a time until you have a big enough staff to execute it. As a person of excellence, as your empire grows, people will call you daily to come help them with a project or partner with them. This is where you will need to know your limit. A good tell-tale sign to know when you're in over your head is when you stop responding to your text messages and emails within 24 hours and start avoiding your phone calls. This is the first sign that you're operating way beyond your capacity and should be an immediate red flag. If you're not moving towards your goal, you are moving away from it.

## 2. Delegate

Every time a person on your team suggests a new idea or project, make them responsible for developing it. If they are the one that came up with the vision and are passionate about it, they should be a much better candidate to complete it and see it to completion. Allow others to explore the possibilities to participate in the growth of your organization.

### 3. Prioritize

Every idea that comes to your brilliant mind isn't for you to complete. It may be for you to complete later after you have more time and money to execute. Some of those good ideas are just a distraction so be careful. In rare cases, if it's a really good idea, make sure you patent, trademark, or copyright it ASAP.

### 4. Know When To Rest And Vacation

I have learned that when you own your own business, you're going to put in more hours working than you ever did working for others. It takes a lot of time, patience, and commitment to sacrifice your weekends and party nights out on the town at the beginning until you become stable enough for the business to run on its own. After this vicious cycle of working hard, some people let the workload take over them and become a workaholic without even knowing it. The main indicator of knowing if you're a workaholic is when:

1. Your schedule includes you working day and nights including your off days.

2. The minute you wake up you reach for your phone to answer emails, and right before you go to sleep you are answering emails.

3. Just the very thought of the little bit of stillness makes you feel like you're being a lazy unproductive couch potato.

To be honest, it's time to pump those breaks. Being a healthy decision maker at work is largely determined by having a well rested mind and well balanced family life. After all, it will be extremely hard to focus and be productive when you know your family is a complete train wreck because of the lack of your presence. Put the phone down at a set time and don't bring business calls in the house if possible. Just because you're at home physically doesn't always mean you're emotionally or mentally there. Plan your vacations and give your body the proper rest it needs to function healthy.

## 5. Family Matters

Sadly to say, after a year's worth of lack of focus, I was forced to close down my business. This is why it is important to know your capacity. Not only was I losing my business, I started losing my family. I had got so busy with chasing my dreams that I forgot about the things that mattered the most to me which was my wife and kids. My intentions were to work hard so that in the near future they wouldn't have to, but it seems as if life had a different plan of storms to shake me up.

As you start to create a high demand for your services, everybody will want to be a part of your team and projects and you will have to know when to say yes and when to say no, as all opportunities aren't good opportunities for your organization. Your business must come first and other organizations come next. Always take care of home first to avoid the same epic failure I experienced that forced me to close my doors.

---

"Gaining success that comes with the price tag of losing your family is not worth it." -Koran Bolden

---

### Balancing Your Quality Time

This section will probably be the three most transparent paragraphs you will ever read on business people who possess a high drive for success and achievement. Most business people I know who are extremely successful are often living and working on building a legacy and great future. But the most challenging part is often scheduling that special now time for our families. Now don't feel bad if this is you because it can be fixed. Our spouse and kids deserve that quality time. They don't care so much about our good intentions on buying the new fancy car, the paid college tuitions, and nice fancy homes with the movie theatre in the man cave. Our kids and significant others really care about us spending that one-on-one time in the process by living in the now.

During this time of me running around and giving my all to help hurting kids and families, I one day felt a heavy conviction that I wasn't attending to my own household with that same love, care, and compassion. This is where things get tricky because as a bread winner we will think everything is ok just because this is the place where you lay your head and put food on the table every night from your hard work. But fatherhood and being a husband is more than that. It's about being a good steward, of managing both business and family at the same time. I quickly recovered from my slip up, and have to often do a check up but in the end it is possible to succeed in business and family simultaneously. Always make spending quality time with the family your #1 priority.

## It Can Happen To The Greatest Of Us

In the Bible this happened to one of the greatest Kings to ever live by the name of King David. King David was the mighty warrior who killed the giant Goliath and was heavily loved by the people in his city. One day David was so focused on winning battles, that he made the big mistake of taking all his soldiers to war and left the women and children unprotected, alone, and vulnerable for an attack. While David and his men were away, the opposing team had planned a sneak attack and kidnapped all the women and kids. When King David and his warriors returned from battle, they all became furious that David had allowed the enemy to overtake their families. In the end, King David got focused and regrouped and eventually rescued everyone who had been kidnapped safe and sound.

The moral of this story is to put some time on your schedule to spend with your family. It is possible to win the battle but lose the war. Who cares about materialistic success and gaining more if at the end of the day you lose everything that really matters the most. Your family is the greatest asset anybody can have.

---

"What you aren't thankful for and appreciate
will eventually evaporate." -Koran Bolden

---

# CHAPTER 16
# BUSINESS LEADERSHIP STYLES

"The leader finds the dream and then the people. The people find the leader and then the dream." -John Maxwell

Now that we know the basics of building a brand, I would now like to identify the 3 main leadership styles that help or harm your business brand. While having a desire to run someone else's business or owning your own business is admirable, understanding where you currently are in your leadership style is much more important. Here are the 3 basic leadership personalities you must understand on your journey to entrepreneurship.

**1.** Followership -The Apprentice Stage

**2.** Leadership -The Spotlight Stage

**3.** Bowsership -The Burnout stage

## A Lesson fromThe Nintendo Playbook

In 1985, one of the greatest video games in the history of the gaming world was created and birth forth a new generation of video game enthusiasts with the culture. This game featured a short, pudgy, fireball spitting, mushroom pouncing lad by the name of Mario. If you have ever played the original classic Mario Brothers game you will become quickly reminded of the storyboard plot of two brothers set on a mission to rescue Princess Toadstool from the antagonizing sharped shelled princess-napping dragon named Bowser.

From all the hype that circulated around its release of this dynamic duo, there were obviously some major differences between these two brothers with surprisingly, two different outcomes. One brother named Mario, was a short overweight thick mustached superhero with enough confidence to get the headlining lead role despite his short man stature that would probably lead the average child smack dab into a bullying situation. But there was something different about Mario. Every challenge he faced throughout the game ended with him defeating King Bowser and stopping him dead in his tracks with victory despite his flaw filled outer appearance.

The other half of the brotherly duo, Luigi, has everything going for himself on the outside with his height, slim weight, and money green outfits. But Luigi is missing something. Luigi seemingly lacks the inward confidence to ever live up to his potential to lead. As the years go on, all the way until the time of this reading, although Luigi is half the reason Mario rescued the princess time after time again, he never got a chance to shine. A few times the creators of the game tried to rebrand Luigi's image and make the consumer buy into Luigi superhero themed games and memorabilia but Luigi's lack of confidence didn't resonate very well with the highly energetic world of gamers. Do you know why? **Here's the answer. So listen closely: Nobody likes to be a Luigi.**

But Why Not?

## 3 Types of People

In the world there are 3 types of people.

1. Followers -Those that watch things happen (Luigi)

2. Leaders -Those that make things happen (Mario)

3. Dictators -Those that hate and oppose the ones who make things happen (Bowser)

Through the past few years, I think I have honestly witnessed each one of these personalities directly have an impact on my life. Dealing with the constant battles of leading my own start up business, I've encountered countless challenges of building customer loyalty and internal staffing issues. You have to know how to properly identify when these personalities are taking place in your organization.

If you plan to take your organization from good to great or from better to best it's going to take some hard work keeping your outlook on life in check. If not, you might end up in the Bowsership category and end up taking your organization down a spiraling tunnel of doom from bad to worse.

## Wrong Myths About Leadership

### Myth #1- *Being a Follower Is For Losers!*

Most people don't like being a Luigi. A Luigi style of leadership is often frowned upon because the man behind the scenes gets no credit or shine time, while the person out front gets all the glory from the team's efforts. Most leaders on this level of leadership often have thoughts of feeling small, insignificant, ignored, and no voice value. But they fail to realize the number one rule of leadership that states that great leaders are first great followers. Just think about it. How can a leader handle the responsibility to step up to the tough challenges that those in a leadership role must face without a guide or coach to mirror?

Far too many times I see people desiring to be a leader ahead of everyone else just to feed their egotistical desires, and end up making more enemies than friends. Overall, the

135

best leaders 9 times out of 10 had the best trainers, coaches, and mentors to help them reach a level that cannot be reached alone.

## Myth #2- I'm Not Qualified Enough To Ever Lead

In life we are called to be a leader at some capacity whether it's situational, or for the long haul but we must be prepared for both. If we are not careful, life's ups and downs can sometimes cause emotional and physical scars that can often lead a Luigi held in his follower-ship position past due his or her time. The problem is not that there are too many people that desire to be a leader, instead I believe the exact opposite. In today's society some have made so many mistakes in life that they are afraid to take the risk of not succeeding. With this limiting belief hovering over them, instead of taking the responsibility of leading many people, they prefer to remain a Luigi forever.

So I present to you today a question that will help some of the readers of this book discover the endless possibilities of what can happen if you truly desire to lead and build your confidence to a level of sky rocketing success and achievement if you honestly take hold of its intent.

If you have been playing the background role for way to long, with all the gifts, talents, and innate abilities you have brewing on the inside of you, why do you continuously desire to be a "Luigi" when you were created to live like a "Mario"?

Luigi: In the background, sidekick, follower, timid, go along with the crowd...

Mario: In the spotlight, leader, head honcho, captain, role model, game changer, trendsetter!

136

It's time for a change! If not, here is what will happen next...

_____

## The Bowser Effect

I don't think anybody ever wants to be a Bowser, or honestly admit that they are currently a Bowser. So to ease up your conviction, I will admit that I have been a Bowser first. Yes, I said it, because being a Bowser is not the problem. Being a Bowser and not being aware that I have become one is the bigger problem. A Bowser is not a bad thing if you catch it and call it for what it truly is. A bowser is a person that knows he should do more, knows he can do more, but is afraid to act in faith and take the steps to do more. They become inwardly bitter because they are so focused on the set back they have to endure versus the things that have gone right in life.

They really begin to go haywire when they see other people that were less talented, and less valuable pass them up, some of which were the ones they helped get started. Instead of continuing to push and press forward, they complain and mope around about everything and become a dark cloud in every room they enter. They end up burning down all their bridges with their bad attitudes and find themselves on an island all alone. This is the state that I was in before I found my purpose in life.

I can honestly say that I have had the pain of going through this phase in life and it almost wrecked my business. I was seeking for a mentor and friends to help me while I was trying to grow my business and nobody would ever go the extra mile with me like I did for them. People who promised to stick with the vision until the end stayed when things were good but hopped ship once things didn't look so promising. I soon became bitter and that bitterness leaked into my marriage, my finances, my business, and friendships. As a visionary you *must* know how to handle betrayal and being overlooked properly in order to succeed.

## How To Develop A Rockstar Team?

"I may not be the smartest, fastest or the most educated man in the world, but that's the least of my worries as an entrepreneur. Although those aren't my main strengths, I am ok as long as I am smart enough to hire someone on my team who is." -Koran Bolden

## The Ball Hog

There once was a high school basketball team that lost every game of the regular season for 3 years straight. Most of the townspeople were astonished at the team's horrific losing streak because the team was handpicked and assembled to become the best team the town had ever seen. To make matters worse, Bobby, the star player on the team had the height, speed, and ability to score 30 points a game, but only when he ball hogged from his teammates.

One day, the parents on the team had become upset with the team's losing streak and signed a petition for the coach to be fired because they hoped that Bobby would be the first player in town to go to the NBA one day. After the new coach was hired, he came in with a fresh mind showing no favoritism to any of the players. His expectations of them were high, and he knew that the key to winning was for them to give their all in a collective effort. Through hard work and perseverance, the team went on to the playoffs for the first time. Surprisingly, this was all accomplished with the star player Bobby sitting on the bench most of the season. As time went on, they eventually won the state championship and they were all offered scholarships to the college of their choice.

In the locker room, the parents and players cheered for joy and poured a bucket of ice cold Gatorade on their coach's head for turning around their team in such a short period of time. Everyone had smiles on their faces accept Bobby. He was furious that he no longer scored 30 points a game. He couldn't believe that his talent was now being viewed equal to his teammates and was very upset that all the players received scholarships. Shortly after, all the players were asked to give a speech of appreciation for the groups collective effort that led to their first big championship, but Bobby refused. With a serious look on his face, Bobby's coach began to correct him for being so inconsiderate. The team knew that Bobby was upset because he didn't get as much shine time as he used to before the new coach came.

He then told Bobby, "Son, there is an old saying that says, that there is no I in team." Then Bobby replied sarcastically, "There may not be an I in team, but there is a me in team." In the end, Bobby was a star player who exposed himself as the culprit that made the team dysfunctional all along. Although he had an amazing talent and a promising future, he stunted the growth of the other player because he didn't believe in teamwork. Bobby was the team's greatest asset and downfall which prevented them from winning in previous years.

## Toxic Waste

Have you ever known someone like Bobby? Do you know someone who had all the talent in the world but their bad attitude and refusal to be a team player prevented them from reaching their full potential. As a business owner, we all want the next big hot shot on our team, but make sure that the motives and attitudes of every person on your team are pure and focused on collective impact. The person who seems like they are the star could be stealing the recognition from your other employees which make them feel like they don't matter. Always do a check up and make a list of who you are giving praise and recognition to. You want your organization to have a balance of team effort and that can't happen if you put all your marbles of praise in one basket. This will cause division. Instead, challenge the star player of your organization to use his influence to motivate the rest of the team. By allowing an inward culture of togetherness to sprout, the team will have a larger since of sticking in for the long haul when things get tough. Motivate your team to be the best they can be and watch your organization turnaround quickly to break new records and win championships.

I seen a great post on social media that will summarize it all. There are 3 types of people in your life:

**1. Who helped you in difficult times**

**2. Who left you in difficult times**

**3. Who put you in difficult times**

## The Pep Talk For Millennials

Here are some simple things you can do daily that will help build your teams confidence and boost company morale. Your team wants the following from you:

| | |
|---|---|
| *New Opportunities | *A Sense Of Belonging |
| *Recognition | *Positive Reinforcement |
| *Results | *Challenging Work Environment |
| *Respect | *No Micro-Managing Zone |
| *Incentives | *A Voice That Matters |
| *Rewards | *A Purpose Bigger Than Self |
| *Trust | *Room To Make Mistakes |
| *Loyalty | *Compassion |
| *Transparency | *Freedom & Fun |

*A Leader Who Can Admit When They Are Wrong
*A Leader Who Keeps His Word
*Coaching That Helps Them Teach Their Full Potential.
*A Coach That Stays At Least Two Steps Ahead Of Them.

# CHAPTER 17
# STREET DREAMZ GRAND RE-OPENING
# PARTY CENTER CONCEPT

"Success "is always under construction." -Steve Harvey
World Renowned Comedian, Author, and TV Host

As you can probably assume, the agony felt from closing my gate for the final time was devastating. After all the work and effort, I would now have to close my doors. Not because of misfortune but because of my lack of experience, leadership, and character to handle the overflow of success. It is true when they say that achieving success is the easy part, maintaining it is truly the hard part.

For the next few days, all I could think about was failing again at my pursuits. The thoughts of me going back to work made me cringe, especially since this time I was failing from success overload. I then began to pray and ask God if this was it. I knew He didn't lead me this far to give up. Then, out of the blue it happened!

My best friend, now wife looked at me and said, "We are not finished, we have just begun." "Huh? I don't understand," I replied. She then took the initiative to draw up a new floor plan to give Street Dreamz an extreme business makeover. Although extremely exhausted and ready to give up, I followed my wife's suggestions and we took the risk of emptying out our complete savings to remodel the business. We then began to announce that we were closed temporarily to remodel although the word around town was that we had failed and closed the shop. We ripped up the old carpet, tore down walls, installed new doors, and upgraded our office furniture. This was a huge leap of faith for my wife and I but we knew we were created to be anything but a failure. In fact, I had the answer to overcome this temporary defeat all along, but this is why it's so important that we keep good people around us because even the mightiest men get weak sometimes. My wife was my guardian angel pushing me through my hardships to make sure the mission was complete. She then reminded me of the mission statement and I got a boost of energy to break out of chains of failure.

## The Elephant that Could-NOT

I once heard of a story that brought this point home for me. One hot summer morning I decided to go to the circus with my family and see one of the biggest most beautiful animals I have ever seen. He was draped in the finest clothing and brilliant enough to accurately perform every command from his master. I thought to myself, "How in the world does this little trainer control a gigantic and powerful animal such as this?" I was left in amazement. As I began to ask around and do my research, I paid close attention to how the elephant was chained down before the performance. This didn't make much sense to me because I have known elephants to be extremely strong in power and great in mind and memory to know that he could surely break free if he wanted to.

After some long research, I found out that although the elephant was stronger and had great power in memory, the trainer outsmarted the elephant. As an infant elephant, the trainer decides to put the shackles around the baby elephant's leg. At that moment, the baby elephant is weak in strength and quickly learns he isn't strong enough to break free. The pain and hurt from the metal shackles begin to implant the limiting belief in the baby elephant that it's totally impossible to break free from the chains. As time goes on, the baby elephant always remembers the pain he endured as a child and never tries to break free ever again. Wow! The trainer found a way to use the strengths and gifting of the elephant's keen memory against him. The same gift that he now gets applauded for at the circus is the same gift that has him stuck inside of shackles.

Just like this elephant that had the power to get out of his circumstances and yesterday's defeat that held him captive all his life, some of us in a similar way, shape or form also possess this limiting way of thinking. These thoughts weigh us down so much that victory is no longer an option and survival is the only way of life. Every day, this mental sickness is currently limiting millions of young professionals from applying for the desired position, owning their own business, enrolling back in school, or even approaching the mate of their dreams to ask for a date. The no's of our past have found a way to make homes in our minds to prevent us from ever receiving the big "YES."

**Testing of my Faith**

"A successful man is one who can lay a firm foundation with the bricks others have thrown at him." David Brinkley

After we started to pull up the carpet, our studio looked a complete mess. Paint was scattered, dry wall was all over the floor, a huge hole was in my wall, while dust flew all around our facility. It was so hideous to look at. After seeing it, I thought we had just made the biggest investment of failure of our life. I couldn't see the vision anymore, but this was the rehab process.

# Spring Cleaning

Anybody who has ever been long overdue for a house cleaning knows exactly what I'm describing. When you finally decide to clean your house, things seem to get worse before it gets better. You find and pull lost stuff from under your bed, clean out cluttered kitchen drawers stuffed with junk mail, you wipe down walls and sweep debris from under tables. After a few short minutes of starting, this once exciting goal of yours has now turned out to be more hard work than what you imagined. But if you continue through with your plans, at the end of your labor you will have a clean room and the peace and clutter free home is worth it all.

When we make mistakes in life or decide that we want to re invent ourselves or upgrade, that means that you are going to have to pull up the old bad habits to experience the new. This means you will have to pull up all the pretty stuff on the outside and have a firsthand look at things happening on the inside just like cleaning a house. It can be horrific to be brutally honest, but in order to get what you never had you will have to go the extra mile.

The reason I decided to write about this process is because I want you to understand that when you decide to move forward and be the best you can be, it's going to cost you something. In fact, in most cases it's going to cost you everything you have. But like my business that was ripped to shreds to improve, we came out on top. Brand new everything! We finally had a second chance to succeed. There were times when I started to doubt if we should invest our last into remodeling, but to quiet those voices, sometimes you have to put your money where your mouth is and act in faith even if it looks as if the odds are all stacked against you. Taking two steps into the future, I'm so glad we acted in faith and decided to invest. We reopened our studio back up even bigger and better than ever before. Our brand stood the test of time and our organization was more respected than ever before.

---

"I use to think that character was defined as what a man did behind closed doors when nobody is watching, but now I know that true character is developed with what a man does in the midst of controversy when everyone is watching with the doors wide open."
-Koran Bolden

---

### Burn The Ships

In 1519, a great example of a man on a mission was Spanish Conquistador Hernando Cortez. One minded Cortez approached the shores of the Yucatan, Mexico with the task of accomplishing what many others had failed to do. He had a great dream to seize the treasures of the Aztec people. The Aztec empire was so superior and had the infamous reputation of being one of the largest and most powerful empires of their time who managed to keep this reigning title of victory for 6 centuries.

With the seemingly suicidal and impossible task before him, and with a much smaller army, Cortez was up for the challenge. Cortez managed to look fear in the face with plans to overthrow the large empire with the rewards of great success, fame, and riches. Through the power of unshakable faith and sky rocketing motivation, Cortez loaded 11 ships with more than 500 soldiers and 100 sailors to set sail from

Spain to Mexico. Then it happened. As the 11 ships approached the Yucatan shore, the all or nothing command of a lifetime left Cortez lips with powerful courage that changed the course of history. Cortez shouted victoriously with a loud roar to his men "Burn the Ships!"

With looks of amazement shifting through the crowd, it was evident that a big problem had been proposed, but Cortez refused to back down even though the odds were stacked against them. He then followed with an even more reassurance that the command he requested was true indeed. "If we are going home, we are going home in their ships." Without a second thought, Cortez and his men burned their own ships they had arrived in. As the story would end, they overthrew the powerful empire of the Aztecs people and went down in history to overthrow 6 centuries of limiting beliefs of other rivals that went before them.

---

### Summary

Similar to Cortez and his men, what limiting belief have you unknowingly picked up on your journey? Whether they are small or great, like Cortez commanded, it's time to burn the ships. From this moment forward you must dare to believe and take on the mentality that nothing can stop you. You must learn to accept the fact that just because others have failed in their attempts, doesn't mean the same applies for you. Cortez knew that the only way for his men to win the battle ahead was for them to take away the option to retreat. I hear so many people say that it seems like every time they try to take one step forward, they end up taking two steps back. Well, good I tell them. Sometimes when you're climbing the ladder of success you have to take a few steps back to see where it is that you're climbing to. This is what happened when we decided to clear out our savings account to revive the business. Once we pulled up the carpet and bought the supplies, there was no turning back. Sometimes no option at all is better than many options. When you have options you tend to procrastinate. When you have no options there is a sense of urgency. You either sink or swim.

# CHAPTER 18
## Overnight Success
## How To Look And Become More Important

A wise man once told me to dress the way I would like to be addressed. So I took his advice and advanced from the block to the boardroom and became an overnight success.
### Koran A. Bolden

"I'm either going down in the history books, or I'm not going down at all." -Koran Bolden

## Making Small Seem Big

Let me ask you a question. What's the difference in the price of a Kia and BMW? They both give you the primary desired goal of getting from point A to point B. So why such a huge difference in price if they both get you to the same place in the same amount of time? The answer is called value proposition. Value Proposition in layman terms is your reasoning of what you cost.

Below are some instantaneous ways to drastically increase your value. In today's market, having the lowest price won't cut it. You will never be able to have a lower price than Walmart. They will put you out of business. You're going to have to give people more than a lower price if you want to make a mark in your industry. Always aim for your products and strive to be the premium luxury brand in the field. Being googleable...

When creating a differential in price, your potential prospects want three basic things. For them to ditch the household name brand items and services that they currently use, you must be able to show if your product is simpler, efficient, or effective. If you can show these three, you can start to really grab people's attention to make the switch.

---

### Entrepreneur Starter Kit

With that being said, here are some starter tools that every entrepreneur needs before they step out in the world of business. This whole list of things could possibly run anywhere between $2500-$5000 on a low end but could produce revenues of 100 times more if you play your cards right. These are especially must haves for those who seek investors for startup capital.

**Website**- There is no higher level of credibility than having a custom made website. Having a website is your virtual 24 hour office space and store front that speaks volumes about who you are and what you offer. Please don't be cheap when it comes to creating a website. Everything else is irrelevant if you don't have a website. So if you're on a tight budget put all your eggs in the one basket and get the other items on this list as you go. A good rule of thumb is that your website should show that your perceived value is eight times more than what you cost.

**Business Cards**- Business cards will be the first thing people ask you for after an introduction. Your cards should be simple and include your name, title, organization, telephone number, website address, and email.

**Demo Video**- Your demo video is a visual demonstration explaining the value of your service or product. They say a picture is worth a thousand words but video is worth a million. Use a professional camera guy to shoot a 2-4 minute video of you in action. Trust me when I say a video will save you a lot of explaining at your meetings.

**Capability Statement**- A capability statement is similar to a business plan but instead of over killing your potential prospects with too much information, a capability statement is direct and straight to the point explaining your business. A good capability statement should be no longer than 5-7 pages. These 5-7 pages should include a cover page, mission statement and objective, a one page bio, what you offer, and recommendation excerpts from industry professionals. The only people who will ever ask for your business plan are investors or an advisory board.

**Proposal-** The #1 question I get from an audience after I speak is how do you properly ask for money or submit a proposal. Having a proposal is critical because if someone asks you for it, that means you are in the running to get what you asked for. When someone asks for a proposal, they are insinuating that you have made a lasting impression on them and they like what they hear. Now the only thing that needs to be discussed is how much does it cost. A proposal can be extensive or simple but for the most part you should try to keep it simple. The proposal is used to justify why spending money with your product or service is going to give them a great return and help their organization succeed greater than before they met you. The bottom line of a proposal is how much does it cost and how is this going to help them.

**Bio/Resume-** This is a no brainer. Your bio/resume should be no longer than 2 pages long and should be justifying why you are the right person for the job. If you are applying for a contract in construction, please don't add things on your bio that don't help build credibility with your awesome work in construction. Your resume and bio should be written to build your case of why you are the best man for the job.

**Presentation-** Sales is the #1 way to get people to buy into your ideas. There are two main presentations that you will need to master if you desire to sell others on your dream. The first is the elevator pitch. So what exactly is an elevator pitch? The elevator pitch says that if you were to get into an elevator on the bottom floor, could you persuade the people on the elevator to buy your product or service by the time you reach the top floor. If you can, your message is concise and clear. However, if you cannot explain your ideas by the time you get to the top floor, you may have a messaging or branding issue and will need to get some help. People that may be able to invest or help are normally very busy people and have a short timeframe to talk. If you master the elevator pitch you get the attention of just about anyone without making the person listening to you feel overwhelmed and unsure of exactly what it is that you're selling.

The second presentation type will more than likely be a Powerpoint or full demonstration of what you have to offer. This gives you a lot more time to explain how your idea works versus the quick and on the go styled elevator pitch. You can use pictures, graphs, charts, quotes, video, visual aids, and written materials to be able to help them understand the full concept on how your product adds value to your potential consumers. But please remember that less is more in todays' fast pace economy where people normally have an attention span of a gold fish. Get to the point, make your message clear, be enthusiastic, smile, and whatever you do, don't sound desperate for a sale. The best way to overcome sounding desperate is to have in your mind that you are willing to walk away from any deal where the potential prospect doesn't get your message fully after your presentation. Know your worth. Stand on your price firmly. Don't cheat yourself by allowing them to get you to lower your price unless they are doing a bulk deal where the more they buy the cheaper the price may be. Any deal that appears you are so desperate that you aren't willing to walk away from is dangerous. The business world can be vicious. If people can't see the value, either walk away, or you may want to spend more time developing your presentation. If your client doesn't see the value in what you offer, it could be that you didn't do such a good job getting them to believe in your value and worth.

Always practice your presentation, upgrade your packaging, and redefine your sales pitch often. Always make sure your message is simple, efficient, and effective.

---

### Making A Lasting Impression In Person

In this chapter, I'm going to cover one of my favorite topics on the subject of charisma. Charisma, or having a likeable personality is one of the most envious traits to have as an entrepreneur. In the church world they call it favor, but whatever you call it, it is a must have if you plan to bust your way through an overcrowded marketplace where everyone is fighting for attention. Some may be thinking that charisma is something that people are born with and there is nothing that they can do about increasing their likeable level, but once again this is completely false. As a person who is naturally introverted mostly due to the fact of losing my brother to a horrific tradgedy, I use to think the same thing. I use to hate the awkward feeling that followed me if I had to meet someone for the first time. My hands would sweat, my knees would shake, and my head would pound just from the thought of meeting someone who was perceived to be more important than me. It got so bad, that for the first two years of business, I refused to attend any meeting without my best friend Rob or my wife LaPortcia being there. That's pretty surprising to some of you who have seen my personality now. The person that was once shy in a room, can now make a grand entrance in any environment I'm in, even if I attend an event solo. Now it's my turn to show you how to look more important so that you get the attention of a room without coming off loud, arrogant, or obnoxious. I'm going to show you how to get people to genuinely gravitate towards you which will make it easier to sell them your ideas later without any clashing.

**#1 Self Worth**- How much you like yourself and respect yourself is how other people will like you and respect you. If you dress raunchy, people will treat you raunchy. If you dress for success, people will treat you like you're successsful. Have a firm handshake, good eye contact, and keep your head up straight.

**#2 Put pep in your step**. Afterall, you are busy right. Busy people have places to go and people to see.

**#3 Be Attentive**- Show up to your meetings with an old fashioned pad and pen to take notes. Using electrical devices could give the misconception that you're working on another project, checking your email, or messaging on social media. Let them know you're focused on them and not other tasks.

**#4 Dress For Success**- Always show up to any event well groomed and dressed to impress. My wife always seems to be more clingy to me when I come home fresh from the barbershop with some clothes on fresh from the cleaners.

**#5 Smell Like Success**- Keep a nice fragrance of cologne or perfume on. Something light and easy. I keep a trademarked cologne that I like to wear because I know that a brand can be associated with smell. The more of the five senses you can attach to your brand, the stronger your brand can become.

**#6 Become A Better Listener**- Whenever you're in an akward moment in conversation, ask a legitimate question and probe for info. If it's one thing I have learned about likability, that's people love talking about themselves, their beliefs, and their ideas.

**#7 Relax**- Unless you're the Queen of England or the baby of Jay Z and Beyonce, nobody starts off being famous. The people you think are important are just normal human beings just like you and I. They make mistakes, have flaws, and have fears just like us all. The good news is that they became who they are through hard work. If you put your hours of labor in, you too can become famous.

## Negotiating Deals

"In negotiation, the most important thing you have to do is to get the other side to respect you." -Donald Trump

Before I go into any meeting there a few things that I must make sure happen before I step a foot in their office. For starters, before any meeting, I make sure I familiarize myself to know the client, and I definitely make sure I do all I can to make sure that they know all about me. This is to make sure that I come onto the playing field with them knowing my worth and how much value I can add to them. Throughout the meeting, I never get straight into business. Getting straight into negotiation shows a lack of concern for their best interest and comes off as being selfish and greedy. So make sure you are prepared to talk about recent events or engage into some cool facts that you found online to break the ice. As you begin to lay out your plans, make sure that the focus of the speech is directed to how you plan to save them money, improve their existing processes, or add significant value to their organization.

Before you get there, do your research. Find out who the key players and decision makers in the building are. Trust me when I say that there are people who influence the decision maker to make their decision on working with you. So treat everybody with respect. For instance, after every meeting I always ask my best friends Rob, Samone, Kevo, and my wife what they think because I know they have my best interest at heart. They can see things that I can't. I make many of my decisions from vibes so sometimes things can seem right at the moment and I want to move, but if I get any resistance from my team I will not move. This is why it is good for you to know and build a rapport with everybody from the CEO to the janitor. You never know who has influence to get the decision maker to buy in.

Another mistake people make in negotiation is that they go into situations not knowing the budget of the prospect. If you don't know their budget, you can potentially under bid or overbid and end up looking like a greedy jerk! Fish around and ask questions indirectly or preferably directly so that you won't waist your time if they don't have the money for you services.

## Knowing When To Talk

When in negotiation, be selective with your words. Don't speak aimless words that don't lead you to solidifying a win/win for both parties involved.

Also, try to avoid acting hard up or desperate. Know your value and be willing to walk away from any deal. Be willing to play hard to get like a man pursuing a women for a date. If you approach a woman who is beautiful but she is too easy, she becomes a turn off no matter how impressive she may look outwardly. All the true power players love obtaining stuff that they can't have so there is no need to keep lowering your price and cutting deals to get them to contract with you. Instead of lowering your cost, spend more time showing why you charge more over your competitors because of your superior service. Don't go too overboard with this because there is such a thing as overbidding. A person who overbids on a contract comes off greedy and unknowledgeable about their industry. Quickly find a common ground and know your walking away point. Establish your worth or else you may walk away with nothing.

## Know How To Be Quiet

What is more important than knowing when to talk, is knowing when to be quiet. I have seen so many people brag on themselves so much in a sales presentation that they end up talking themselves out of a deal. I found that the one who talks the most in a meeting is often the one who is normally full of crap and loses out. They have learned to talk a good game but when it comes time to execute their hasty dealings end with them being the ones who normally come in last place. All bark, no bite! Always try to under commit but over deliver. You don't need to outshine others to validate your value.

# CHAPTER 19
# WORKING WITH BANANA REPUBLIC

"The secret to success is that there is no secret to success.
Just do what you love." -Oprah Winfrey

It's amazing that when I first envisioned opening a recording studio that would help young people make healthy life choices, that I never expected all these new opportunities to show up at my doorstep. I went from being a local urban rapper to a highly respected businessman and community outreach mogul. Never in a million years did I ever think that I would be wearing suits and ties and sitting in business meetings negotiating major deals with Fortune 500 companies.

## Chandra Taylor

For me to say that I have become who I am today by myself would be totally disrespectful and a complete overstatement. No one gets to the top of the high rise ladder without someone holding the bottom legs of the ladder in position. I have learned that different people come into our lives through different seasons for different seasons to make little small deposits in our bucket of success. One person may show you how to deal with hate, while another may show you how to properly love. Collectively, these people come together to show us how to behave and make decisions in life, so it's best to keep those around you that have your best interest at heart.

One of those people who showed me how to present myself as a first class businessman was a woman by the name of Chandra Taylor. When I first met Chandra, she was polite, full of energy, and passionate about seeing her customers succeed. Since her store was located in the same mall that I had my recording studio, I would often stop by her store to see what was the latest fashion trends from her Banana Republic store. Through out the years, my career started to blow up in the business world, and so did she. She went from being a store manager to a general manager through the years that I had known her and it was exciting to often share our success stories with one another.

---

## The Cadillac Ad

In the fall of 2013, I received a phone call from a friend of mine by the name of Julie from Saint Louis Magazine who asked me if I would be interested in an amazing opportunity to be featured as a Cadillac City Shaper. They would feature

my wife and I for the work that we do with young people.
They had been following our story and thought it would be
perfect to showcase our success in a full page spread with a
new Cadillac car that had just been announced for release.
So you know what my answer was right? YES!!!!!!! LaPortcia
and I immediately went to meet with Chandra and her store
to get an outfit for our first magazine ad.

Two months later, the magazine released on the news
stands and I decided to deliver a copy personally to Chandra
with a hand written letter thanking her for showing me how to
dress for success. She was in total awe after seeing the
Cadillac ad that she personally help dress me for and had no
idea that she had such an impact on my life after reading the
thank you letter. Here is a copy of that letter:

# Letter To Chandra

My name is Koran Bolden, a national youth motivational speaker and entrepreneur who advocates for kids to graduate from school on time.

Just three years ago, I was a young man who had no interest in putting on a suit and tie or blazer jacket. I wore baggy clothes and baseball caps that caused more hurt to my brand as a business owner than helping it.

That all changed once I met a Banana Republic Factory store associate by the name of Chandra Taylor. She was polite, professional, and helped me try on my first blazer. When I looked at myself in the mirror, my confidence immediately shifted to higher heights. Not only did I begin to look like a young professional, I began to walk, talk, and act like one as well.

At my meetings, I started to receive compliments on my clothes and people started to treat me differently. My business soon flourished and thanks to your store, I have become a city-wide respected entrepreneur and youth advocate for building future business leaders.

Since then, I have been featured in news stories, and have spoken to more than 30,000 youth. Chandra saw beyond the old me, choosing to focus her energy and expertise on the person I could become. She showed me weekly how to present myself as a young person of respect and influence. In media publications where I've been featured, I have always modeled the Banana Republic brand and I feel like I'm embedded in the culture of fashion, professionalism, respect, and honor.

Thank you for allowing me to represent the new fashion statement of Young America from Banana Republic.

*Koran Bolden, Youth Motivational Speaker and CEO of Street Dreamz Recording Studio*

## The Attitude Of Gratitude

I once heard a wise man ask the question, "What if you wake up today, with only the things you thanked God for yesterday?" If that question was made into a statement and became universal the world would be truly a better place. So often we are so focused on the things that seem like big problems in our life that we hardly pay attention to the things that are a big blessing to us. We have the power to change the world with a simple thank you. That thank you letter was forwarded to Chandra's regional manager and was read aloud on the next conference call. I was happy that Chandra got the recognition that she had deserved. This letter was perfect timing because Chandra had just got promoted to general manager. I was happy to write a letter that confirmed that they had made the right decision with her promotion.

---

## The Thank You Letter Heard Around The World

One morning I decided to get up early in the morning and read some affirmations. Honestly, I was feeling kind of grumpy and was overloaded with some heavy anxieties with taking the business to the next level. I was truly at a low moment in my life, and so I did the best thing I could think of which was to meditate myself into a realm of pure gratitude and vision.

Then it happened! After sitting in complete stillness, I felt that something good was about to happen to me. Once I get this feeling, I know that means something good is truly happening behind the scenes that I cannot see for my good, and all I have to do is trust and believe that intuition and confess it out my mouth as if it has already happened. So I spoke out loud, "Something good is going to happen for me today." As I walked downstairs in full expectation to receive what I confessed, I picked up my cell phone to check my email, and to my surprise something amazing happened that I could have never dreamed, thought, or imagined. It was an email from the corporate headqaurters saying that they recieved my thank you letter and read about how wearing their Banana Republic brand helped me achieve success and wanted to feature my story on the Gap Inc website! I couldn't believe it. Gap Inc., receives millions of letters all year long and they find mine like a needle in a haystack and decided to post it on their global site? Wow! What happened then blew my mind.

Once I spoke with the corporate office about the post, I posted it on my social media sites and they did as well. My city was truly proud of this huge accomplishment, and tons of comments flooded the Gap website within 2 days. They emailed me and told me that they had never received this many comments on a blog post and were really excited about the story. The lady over the blog post then tells me that since the story resignated with people on line, that they had decided to plaster the blog post on their internal server, where every person who logged into the main system would have to see it as soon as they logged in. What that meant was that my letter of appreciation would now be read in the US, Canada, Japan, and Europe. My story had gone global from a simple thank you letter to a store associated who was just doing her job which was to make her customers feel more confident and happy. After the post on the internal site, tons of comments started to pour in from general managers from all across the globe. They were excited to hear that their orgaization was doing more than selling clothes, but giving some of their customers a fresh start to fulfilling their dreams. And just when you think this story couldn't get any better, it does.

The next day, I was leaving school and noticed I had another email from a man by the name of Dan Leavitt. Dan was from the global headquarters of Banana Republic and decided to email me after seeing my story on their internal server. He was contacting me to see if I would be interested in a opportunity of a lifetime by flying my wife and I to Las Vegas to speak on stage in front of 1000 Banana Republic general managers from across the world. My mouth dropped! "Dan, I'm lost for words. I don't know what to say. Wow," I humbly shouted on through the phone. My heart was beating so fast that I could literally feel it pulsating through my chest.

"That's right, we have decided to fly you and your wife both to Las Vegas and will always have you come in style. We have arranged for you and your wife to meet with a stylist at one of our stores for a full fledge shopping spree at our store to pick out a few outfits of your choice," Dan replied. From that day forward, I experienced the possibilities that come from what sometimes feels like impossible circumstances. Just a few days ago I was drowning in my business full of worry, and then in a matter of a few hours the verdict of failure had been served with an eviction notice for removal from the premises. My wife and I accepted the offer, met with a stylist, and picked an  amazing attire for our trip to Las Vegas. What an amazing story to share with you all! When all the cards are stacked against you, you can believe your way out of trouble.

## The Bellagio Hotel

After our plane landed in the city of lights, we approached the baggage claim and noticed a man holding a sign with the last name Bolden on it. He greeted us with a smile and amazing hospitality while informing us that the good people from Banana Republic requested a special limosine service to take us to our hotel at the beautiful Bellagio hotel. LaPortcia hopped inside the limo with the biggest smile on her face that I had ever seen. It was as if she was giving me the big pat on the back as her husband while confirming that she was proud of me as a father, husband and visionary. That million dollar smile is still imprinted in my head until this day. All the long years of her being by my side and helping me with the business without any guarantees of a reward at the end of the road had to be tough. It requires a lot of trust to follow a play based on nothing but a plan that was developed by faith. But she stayed true and loyal and we were now in Las Vegas on an all expense paid trip by Banana Republic.

## The Big Rock, Paper, Scissors Philosophy Debuts

I woke up early on the day of the conference to go practice my big speech that I was to deliver in a few hours. I was excited and relaxed but eager to get it over with. As the big moment approached, I was sitting back stage in the director's chair praying that my message be received well with the corporate audience. One of my big dreams was to have my speech translated in different languages to the audience, and guess what There was a translator in the back who translated everything I said in Japanese for the Banana Republic Japan team. The moment for me to speak had now arrived. "Now coming to the stage, Koran Bolden," said the person introducing me. I then snapped into my zone and delivered an amazing speech. By the time I was done, I didn't know how a corporate crowd at this magnitude would receive a speaker with an urban hip hop rags to riches story, but I did my best. As I walked back stage I was embraced by the media team with tears and hugs. As I looked at the backstage monitors I then saw people giving me a standing ovation for my speech. I went back out, took a bow and received many praises for a job well done.

I had the opportunity after the event to meet many people from all over the world who informed me just how much my story had impacted their life. They appreciated my true authenticity and some said I was the best speaker of the entire three day conference. From that day forward, I truly understand what it means when people say always be yourself. Instead of being like someone else, I had made the right decision to be myself and that's what made my speech become highly praised with a standing ovation. That was one of the best experiences of true identity I have learned so far in life.

## Summary
Before I went to Vegas, I hired a speech coach to help me prep for the event. I thought it would be a good idea to get some advice on how I could effectively communicate on the corporate level. When she asked to hear my speech, she told me it was horrible. She said that I was very passionate but my tone comes off too urban. She wanted me to be more like other speakers in elequent speech because it would open up more opportunities to go global than if I spoke how I currently did. Honestly, I took her advice to heart because she was a so called expert in the field of speech and grammar.

Over the next few weeks, I tried over and over to practice speaking how she advised but something wasn't right. Although I understood that her intentions were to show me how most African American men advance in the world through advanced vocabulary, I felt as if I was coming off being unauthentic. I kept looking at myself in the mirror feeling like I was losing my identity and brand that everyone loved as a speaker. On the day of the event, I made the decision to scrap her advise and be the best me I could be. Hate it or love it.

I could have gone on stage and delivered my speech like my ex-speaking coach suggested me to do, but I chose to be myself. What gave me the confidence to reject her advice is because I had given hundreds of speechs before where people told me I was one of the best speakers that they had ever heard. So why change my recipe for success.

---

### This Can Happen For You Too!

When you get serious about your craft through hard work, dedication, and consistency you are now in a perfect position to handle the blessing when it presents itself. The opportunity for me to speak showed up when I became thankful, and when my practice and preparation aligned. Sometimes things don't happen as fast for us because we are not ready. If I would have had this opportunity two years ago I wouldn't have been ready. I had been practicing my Rock, Paper, Scissors speech hundreds of times for free long before anybody ever paid me a dime to start speaking for money. If you really believe in your dream, prepare today as if your big opportunity will happen tomorrow.

## CHAPTER 20
## KORAN BOLDEN DAY
## MARCH 21, 2014

"There are two types of people who will tell you that you cannot make a difference in this world: those who are afraid to try and those who are afraid you will succeed." -Ray Goforth

This chapter will be short and sweet. I think by now you get the point that success happens only on your level of belief, planning, and focused work ethic. The part that I would like to discuss in this chapter is something I call social capital.

If you ask any banker or experienced business man, they will tell you that most businesses fail because of their lack of financial capital in the bank. Financial capital is the life line of your business when a bad month of sales come hitting you like a ton of bricks. The capacity of money or assets that you have in reserve determines how long you will be able to stay in business until sales pick back up. If you don't have any money in the bank, you will be forced to close down shop.

## What Is Social Capital?

---

"Your network, is largely associated with your net worth!"
-Author Unknown

---

Social capital is similar to financial capital but involves people as your assets instead of money. The depth of the relationship you have with people in your industry largely determines how successful you will be in life.

The Law of Reciprocity says that when you do things for others, they feel obligated and compelled to do things for you. This is why adding value is the main ingredient for a person that wants to be rich in the social capital arena.

It's really simple. Let's say for instance that you want 100 people to show up to your 21st birthday party. The average person would probably start sending out invitations and reminders 2-4 weeks before their big celebration which is probably too late for them to hit their desired goal. They should have started a year ago.

Social capital is about deposits and withdrawals. If you add a lot of value to people, then when you make a request they are more likely to return the favor. It's common courtesy in American culture. The more you have in your social bank account the more favors you can request.

"The reason that people have so little support with their dreams is because they do little to nothing to support other people's dream."
-Koran Bolden

## Going Bankrupt

On the classic game Wheel of Fortune you see game show contestants spinning a wheel hoping to walk away wealthy, rich, and with a ton of cash. One of my pet peeves with this game is when you see someone who has all the cues to solve the puzzle, but instead they keep spinning the wheel and end up landing on the bankrupt sign and end up losing it all.

An example of a person who goes socially bankrupt is a person who keeps asking people to borrow money and never lends. Or a person who continually has these so called special events every other month. They want you to come to their birthday party, their kids party, their kids Bar Mitzvah, their anniversary dinner, the kids birthday party, and all other sorts of shindigs. If you keep having these special events every month, you're setting yourself up for great disappointment when you plan a big event and nobody shows up. You have exhausted all your social capital. Try to be considerate and keep your request down to a minimum so then when you have a big event, it will look like you're the man or woman of the hour with all your people supporting you at one time. Be very strategic with your request. I always look at it like I'm in the woods hunting with only one bullet in the gun. I have one shot to get what I truly want.

This perfectly sums up the laws of adding value. If you're not solving problems for people, you're eventually going to lose them out your life.

## Connecting the Dots

Another great thing that I want to bring to your awareness is that it's important to avoid conflict with people at all cost. There will be some people that you have disagreements with but this shouldn't be a habit or everyday pattern in your communication. You never know who know's who. You could be arguing with someone in a grocery store, not knowing that the person you are arguing with is the son of the business that you're trying to gain a partnership with. Do you think he is going to refer you? If you said yes, please think again.

## Koran Bolden Day

In the last chapter I explained how I was presented with the wonderful opportunity to speak at the Banana Republic conference through building a relationship with the general manager Chandra Taylor. What I didn't tell you is that the story goes deeper than me writing a letter and flying to Vegas. I was able to make a phone call through a friend of mine and request for Chandra to be awarded with a proclamation from Saint Louis County and for Chandra to have her own day for the outstanding community service work she did with me and other young people. Chandra was just doing her job and probably never knew how much of an impact she had on my business and staff, but this was my opportunity to repay her back for always believing in me, and teaching me how to get others to believe in me by dressing for success. So how was I able to make a phone call and grab the attention of Saint Louis County Executive Charlie

Dooley? I had social capital with a great woman by the name of Ms. Pat Washington.

Ms. Pat has to be one of the most powerful women I have ever met. If she sees an injustice, she will literally stop whatever she is doing and defuse or correct any situation. What's important about this story is that I use to mentor her son Young Prince in my recording studio for 3 years. When I first met her she worked for the Saint Louis County Health Department. She would always encourage me to keep shooting for the stars and tell me thanks for mentoring her son to greatness. Who would have thought that 3 years later Ms. Pat would be promoted to be the assistant to the most powerful man in the Saint Louis County Government

After the media started to pick up on our story of how a hometown hero was working with Banana Republic, I made a phone call to her and asked if a proclamation could be made for Chandra Taylor as a thank you for her amazing customer service. She replied, "Of course Koran. You have mentored so many young people in our city including my son, and I would be more than happy to help you fulfill this request.

Over the next few days, we decided to plan a surprise media pop up on Chandra in a Banana Republic store. She had no idea what we were up to, but she was about to be presented with one of the biggest awards a person can receive in the city.

We all gathered on a Thursday afternoon, and yelled surprise to Chandra as her store employees shouted with joy. With the cameras rolling, Chandra gave a speech that rocked the house. She spoke on the fact that she was just doing her job. She was following the Banana Republic mission statement which states that they do more than sell clothes. When I bought my first Banana Republic blazer, Chandra did just that. She not only sold me a blazer, she sold me confidence, integrity, self esteem, and boldness. I received all of this, not because the jacket alone gave me this, but because the blazer jacket mixed with love and belief in her customers is what made the impact on my life.

Lastly, shortly after Charlie Dooley gave her a proclamation and declared March 21, 2014 as Chandra Taylor Day, he then turned to me with a huge smile on his face. I started to think in my head, "What's going on?" but like the old saying goes, what goes around comes around. Charlie Dooley decided to surprise and acknowledge me for my community leadership work in the areas of entrepreneurship and youth empowerment. I couldn't believe it. A good act that I had arranged for someone else had come back upon me. Now I have a proclamation that reads Koran Bolden Day on March 21, 2014. What an amazing story to tell of how small communities can come together to make a big difference.

Here is what I would like to leave you with.

**1.** You never know who people will become, so be kind to people in power, people who are on their way up and people who seem to have no power at all. I was just doing my job and mentoring a young man who had the potential to be great in life. I never knew his mother would be in a position to fulfill a proclamation request. A good name and reputation can only be achieved by adding value to others.

**2.** Chandra was just doing her job. She wasn't fighting to be seen, dealing with office politics, or begging for awards. Chandra Taylor was simply operating her area of giftedness and doing what she loved to do and success found a way to her doorstep in the most unorthodox way she could imagine. When you're doing your job, even if your boss or customers never acknowledge you that doesn't mean you're worthless. Just keep doing your job and putting your best foot forward and one day you will eventually get your big pay day and recognition openly for the world to see.

## Where People Drop The Ball

I would now like to briefly touch on how some people quickly go bankrupt in the world of social capital. If you commit any of these violations, I will promise you that you will build up bridges and burn them down just as quickly. You will never make it to the top and stay there.

**Prideful**- Some people are too prideful to ask for help. Women often have been told by their moms to become independent and to never rely on a man for anything. Men have often been disappointed by men so much to the point that they would rather fail than to feel the hurt and pain from disappointment ever again. Wake up and shake it off! Some people may experience getting 100 no's, but who care's as long as at the end of the journey you get that one special yes.

**Wait Too Late**- When people finally decided to ask for help they wait until the last minute when they are too far deep in trouble for anybody to be able to get them out of a jam.

**Selfish**- These people only call you when they need something and in the event that you need help from them, they make you jump through fire hula hoops to return the favor. Some refuse to return the favor all together.

178

**Unappreciative**- You can help them out the worse of situations, but they never say thank you beyond words. They never check to see how you're doing after you have helped them. They never write you a letter or send a simple text to check and see if you're still alive.

**Unstable**- They never maintain relationships. They are so busy with dealing with their life struggles that they can barely take the time out to return phone calls or texts. You can help these people a million times and they still come back asking for more due to their poor decision making which keeps them from getting ahead.

**Competitive**- They are happy for you and want you to do good as long as you don't do better than them.

**Debbie Downers**- Always complaining, negative, and nagging. Nothing ever pleases them. Nobody likes being around them because they will suck the life out of the party.

**The Self Sabotager-** This is the person who wants to move forward in business but thinks they will get there alone. They have been hurt by so many back stabbing friends, employees, colleagues, and associates that they can't function in the area of trust. But trust and communication is the foundation of leadership. They are their own worst enemy.

### Summary

If you want to be a person of high success, become a server and put others before yourself. For three years I gave up my Wednesdays and Sundays just to serve as a youth leader at my church. I wasn't getting paid, and I had nothing to gain other than doing a great service. But serving them kept my heart pure and made me feel like I had a purpose in life. I had the great privilege of sharpening my speaking skills, and even received the mentoring of the two greatest youth directors on the planet named Mark and Nikki Supak. My Church on the Rock kids gave me a reason to add value and share my gifts and understand how much my time could change the lives of others. Adding value to others is true success.

Barack Obama is a perfect example of a person who gained success and made history by becoming the first African American President of the United States. In his second election term, he ran against Mitt Romney who drastically raised more money than Obama which should have literally bought him the majority of the election votes. But connections with people always triumph over money. People want to support a person that has their heart. It goes back to the good ole saying that money can't buy you love.

Determine this day that you will step out the box and be intentional about managing your current relationships while slowly building new ones. The last suggestion is this. Building true authentic relationships happen over time and shouldn't be rushed. It may take years to build a relationship with true substance and depth, and just like with a bank account, make sure you put in more than you take out and you will become a person of great influence.

# CHAPTER 21
# HOW TO TAKE YOUR BRAND NATIONAL

"Either write something worth reading or do something worth writing." -Benjamin Franklin

This chapter is specifically for those who want to take your brand on a higher platform. I will be brief, so pay attention. The reason that I won't spend too much time on this topic is because I don't want you to focus on being seen. That's the #1 for sure way to stay local. People who want to be famous and seen just for the sake of being famous to be seen are losers. They will never make it in the world of global impact because their focus is only on helping themselves. Their social capital remains in a negative balance. These people have a bad reputation and the sad part is most of them don't even realize it until their brand has been so drug through the mud that it's become irreparable. So I dedicate this chapter instead to those who have a solid foundation and would like to build their resume only to be seen to move their cause or company forward to get more traction.

## The Day I Realized I Wasn't Normal

I remember like yesterday the first time I thought to myself that there was something special about me. Not in some arrogant egotistical manner, but in a manner that comes from and inner state of humility mixed with passion that makes you believe that it is truly possible to change the world and leave it better than you found it. It was hard to accept the fact that I just might be the next young person from my city to grasp the torch of cultural leadership. After all, I was introverted and shy when I first met people years ago. I had made so many mistakes that I didn't think I could ever be used. But those were all lies that I was telling myself. The truth is, some of the biggest losers end up becoming the biggest winners, and some of the biggest winners end up being the worst losers.

As I stood up for what I believed and allowed my struggles to help me build patience, news stations, radio stations, magazines, and corporations started to give me rave reviews for my community outreach. I couldn't believe it, but after I ran from this position for the first couple of years in business, I soon stepped up to the plate despite all my flaws and shortcomings. If you want to go global fast, I am going to highly suggest that you keep your image clean. Excessive drinking, smoking, displayed forms of raunchiness and potty mouthing off in public could potentially rub some people the wrong way. In the area of media and business partnerships it's all about referral. If one person works with you and you show yourself to be professional, prompt and valuable, they will refer you to their circles of friends in the same industries.

When people refer you, they are putting their official stamp on you. This is something that should not be taken lightly. A person giving you a referral means that they have a high trust level that you will deliver a superior service to their family and friends and so it's best to be on your best behavior. If word gets around that you dropped the ball and could not deliver an exceptional product or service, you will quickly tarnish your brand.

Most television media outlets call me because I was referred by their friends. Eventually, these people became my friends and they referred me to their friends. Do you see the cycle? I now have dozens of people in my phone that I can call at the drop of a dime if I need to get on TV, and that's not because I'm the most talented person in the world or the only person in my field who does what I do. It's because I treat everybody with the utmost respect from the camera man to the TV host. My main goal when I enter a room or meet people is to make an impression that I am the best man for the job. I work on myself daily by asking myself how can I make my personal relationships and friendships unforgettable experiences.

## How To Get On TV

Most people honestly have PR companies to get them on TV. I would strongly suggest that every business start off with a good PR company because they are experts in making your message precise and focus formats for the media to accept your story. We must always remember in the media that there is so much news breaking that you only have a few seconds to grab the television producers attention. They don't have time to read your bio, view your website, or listen at your long conversations. Their goal as a media company is to get news out quicker than their competitors in the social media age. Their shows make money by selling ads and their overall influence based on their ability to keep people's attention as a credible source to break news which gains them followership. The more followers, the more corporations buy ads, the more profit they make. Not only are they competing against other TV stations and media outlets, they are also competing with social media who often break news first. This is why it's important to get a PR person. They will help you get the point across quickly. PR people have long lasting relationships that you don't have right now. You are essentially buying their relationships from them.

After booking a good PR you must be able to execute effectively on the following:

**Be Available**- Media outlets only have a small window to push out good content. If they need a story and you're not ready, the show must go on.

**Speedy Reply-** If a TV show producer contacts you by way of text, phone, or email, please make sure you respond ASAP. If you don't have all the pictures, info, or details they are requesting please still respond and let them know. Lack of communication makes the person creating the story deem you as non-credible. They will never ask you for an interview again.

**Know Your Stuff-** Strive to be an expert in your field and learn to give quick direct answers to their questions. If it takes you longer than one minute to reply to a question, you may need to focus your message down a bit more. Most media outlets want you to get straight to the point with interesting stuff. Make sure your answers to their questions are enthusiastic and in the form of an elevator pitch. Simple but efficient.

**Have A Following-** The news stations of course have their own followings, but you become even more of an asset if you have your own following to help them make your story go viral. If you have a social media fan base, always engage those people who are following to repost and get the word out. Those views and reposts go into their database and if you get a great response, who do you think they will call when it's time to cover a similar story in your field? Start working on your social media followers to advocate for you when you start hitting the media world. They are free word of mouth for your business.

**Be Googleable-** Trust me when I say that social media is the first place people look as their number 1 reference choice to see who you really are. Everybody on the planet earth fills out their flawless job resumes, and if you read them you would think this potential employee could do nothing wrong. But think again. If you were to hire them and you wait just a few months later, the real "them" starts to show up on the scene. On their resume they claimed that their greatest strength was their ability to be prompt, but three months later they are on their final warning to get fired because of excessive tardiness. They put on their resume that they work better in an environment that deals with multi-tasking, but six months later they are totally stressed out with a stack of overdue projects cluttered on their desk. This is why employers don't give two cents about a resume anymore. They would rather go straight to the source, your social media page.

Employers understand that who you truly are will reflect with what you continuously write about. If you say you're honest and full of integrity but your social media site shows you getting drunk and wild at all the local bars, do you think that your resume will be a more credible source than a place where you share thoughts and ideas on social media? Make sure that your social media and google lookups are on point, because social media and google is the highest ranking resume that one can have when building a brand.

## The Successful Failure Interview

I can remember a time a few years back when I had a job interview that I nailed perfectly. The interview went so well, that my interviewer stop asking me business questions and starting asking questions insinuating that I had the job. She asked if I could step outside for a moment while her team deliberated. I quickly pardoned myself. As I sat in the call center, on-looking floor employees kept whispering to me that they knew I had the job. They informed me that when you make it to the second interviewer it's a done deal. I felt really good about the interview process and so I started to feel relaxed until the next interviewer came out of her office with a different demeanor on her face and quickly asked me to leave the premises. "Thank you for your time Mr. Bolden, but we have decided that we will pass on your employment here," she replied. On the way to the car I wondered if there was something I did that made the woman upset. Later that day, I found out through the temp agency that set up the interview, that while I was waiting in the lobby, they were busy looking at my activity on social media sites. They stated my social media sites didn't match the person I was on my resume and they didn't think I would be a good fit for their company. Please be aware that your social media sites and website must match the viewpoints of the position that you want to get hired for and the companies that you want to partner with. If you say you have a strong community outreach and you want to work with kids, posting weekend pictures of you at the bar getting sloppy drunk doing belly shots may suggest that you are an irresponsible party animal and may not be the best role model for dealing with kids. To make a long story short, keep your personal life personal and never post anything you would want to delete later.

## How to Partner with Corporations?

Don't be thirsty for partnerships. Always remember that all corporations first started out just like you did, small with nobody believing in them. Be so great that they want to connect into your relevance and creativity.

Whenever you're about to enter into a partnership or choose a team, ask yourself if you had unlimited resources would you still do business with them. Does the brands reputation add value to you or align with your current mission statement? Don't go off trying to seek partnerships with big brands just because it looks good. Being exclusive says that your brand is high in value. If everybody can work with you, nobody will want to work with you. You will become a trend and play out in the long run.

## How To Find Investors?

Most investors will only work with people who can show financial statements that their product or service already is a proven method. This is why it's important for you to keep track of every dollar you spend from day one by making frequent deposits in the bank. Investors like to see proven systems that work that just need capital to enhance their business. Most investors are only interested in business models that have financial statements or have valuable ideas linked with exclusive patents and trademarks. The only other way to solidify a business idea is through social capital and demonstration. This means that you present your ideas in a showcase or have a great connection with a person who doesn't mind taking a risk. But that will come down to how much they trust you so make sure you have a wealthy social connection with that person before you make the ask.

There are angel investors out there as well that may invest in your good ideas but the less information that you have that this product has sold before, the stronger you will have to demonstrate and convince the investor how this product will give them a return on their investment.

"If you haven't made a significant investment in your business, why would anybody else want to invest in your business?"
-Koran Bolden

## CHAPTER 22
## DEATH OF THE VISION BOARD

"Success usually comes to those who are too busy
to be looking for it." -Henry David Thorea

"What in the world is wrong with you Koran?" This is what
most audience members say when I tell them to trash their
current vision boards. The confused look on their faces tickle
me on the inside as if I just rained on their parade with all
their hopes and dreams of finally achieving the extravagant
homes, cars, road to fame cut out in small little pieces from
the latest magazine now plastered with glue on a fresh white
vision board. For those that aren't familiar, a vision board
has been suggested by many motivational speakers and law

of attraction leaders as the single source to attracting your wildest dream to come into fruition. While I do believe in the law of attract and do believe that your body acts on the most dominant images that you keep in front of you, I must bring something very important to your awareness, so listen closely. Read this next line really slowly 10 times out loud so you don't miss what I am about to tell you.

**Money and materialistic things can never fill the void inside your heart and make you feel whole.**

If this is the case, why do we spend so much time cutting out big airplanes and jets out of magazines to put on our visions boards as if they will add value to who we are. The truth is that you are valuable whether you achieve these temporal things are not. In fact, you were of great value even before the day that you were born.

---

"Before I formed you in the womb I knew you, before you were born I set you apart; I appointed you as a prophet to the nations." Jeremiah 1:5

---

To put so much value on these material things as our ultimate goal is a false sense of self. What happens if you don't ever achieve the monetary success that will eventually lead to you driving home the brand new Bentley to park in your 5 story home to park it in your 5 car garage with the pool in the back? Would you say that your life would be a failure or that you were insignificant? I sure do hope not. Well, if that's the case, then why are our vision boards 80 percent filled with reaching for things that we want instead of being *thankful* for the things we already have been given. Think about that for a moment.

What I am about to say next will totally change your life and knock so many years of stress and decades of labor off your life that you will never be the same if you receive this simple over looked method to attaining success. There is one thing more powerful than creating a vision board, and that's to create a victory board. Listen closely, they both have power to create wealth and success for you, so by no means am I saying that a vision board is false. What I am saying is what does it profit a man to gain the whole world but lose a sense of self? Here the major difference of creating a vision board and creating a victory board.

---

**A Vision board is about you chasing success...**
**A Victory board is about success chasing you....**

---

Let me explain...

There was a story in the bible about a man named Solomon. His dad was King David who defeated the giant named Goliath and became one of the greatest Kings to ever live. When his dad had passed away, he was a little worried that he had to fill the shoes of his father who was great in war and loved deeply by the people. One day, God appeared to Solomon in a dream to confirm that He would be with him just as He was with his father. To confirm the validity of this statement, God asked Solomon to ask for whatever he wanted, and He would grant him whatever he desired. Most people would immediately grab their vision board and get to rambling things off their list as if it was a Christmas gift. They would be eager to be successful, famous, and in the spotlight to make sure they adequately filled the shoes of their father.

Instead of asking for riches and honor, he asked God for the gift of discernment, to know the difference between good and evil so that he could properly lead God's people in righteousness and justice. To bring this point home, Solomon even gave thanks to God for being such a great guide to his father David before he made his request for a righteousness judgement in his new leadership role. Solomon was not focused on getting more, Solomon was focused on being thankful for what he already had. So what did God reply to this humble request?

See, thanksgiving for what you already have is greater than what your'e about to get. I think Solomon knew how to move the hand of God after reading his Father King David's book of Psalms where he often praised and thanked God even though his enemies were out to kill him. He often thanked God for defeating his enemies even while all the cards were stacked against him and it looked as if there was no way out.

---

"Faith properly works at it's zenith capacity
when it is preceded by the ambassador of thankfulness."
-Koran Bolden

---

To be honest, I have never created a vision board. Sure I write my visions down, and sure I desire to have the brand new Ferrari sitting in my driveway one day, but that's not more important to me than my family, my mom, my sister, my kids, my nephew, my hunger to impact youth, or my drive to see a modern day revival for our nation to wake up and lives its full potential. It is my belief, that God is the same today, yesterday, and forever and so if Solomon didn't have to ask for riches and he became the richest man in the world to date, why do I?

In the bible it says that you have not because you ask not. Most people read that scripture and stop reading, but if they only read the next line. It says that you have not because you ask not, and when you ask, you do not receive, because you ask with wrong motives, that you may spend it on your pleasures.

What that means is that if you want to get rich to show everybody just how good you look, you have the wrong motives and will never have it. And if you do get to obtain it, it will come with many sorrows.

There is another time in the scriptures when Jesus walked into a city where 10 people stood outside the city gates as outcast because they had leprosy. Jesus walked into town and had compassion on them and healed them. As they left blessed and healed only one person took the time to come back to say thank you for their healing. When Jesus heard this, he asked the man that gave thanks where were the other 9 lepers that he healed? Why didn't they thank the man that just gave them a normal life again? But what proceeded out the mouth of Jesus next changed my life forever once I read it. He said to the healed man that since you have come back and have given thanks to God be healed and made whole.

"What?" You mean to tell me you can be blessed without being whole and full on the inside?" I thought to myself. The answer is yes! Blessing and materialistic things can be obtained but having a thankful heart is the only thing that can make you feel whole and significant. I didn't mean to turn this into a bible study but I want you to learn first hand how you can be in a position where you lose your family, house, and cars trying to grab for more. Chasing success itself can lead to greed if we're not careful. Lastly, once you do have thanksgiving in your heart, you will then receive the proper vision and I can assure you it has nothing to do with buying planes, helicopters, and big jets. Sure it's ok to desire nice things, but life is so much bigger and meaningful when your vision is about being thankful for what you already have and developing a vision that helps build up the value of others.

---

"A victory board is a daily reminder that all things are still possible when it looks impossible to catch up and win." -Koran Bolden

---

## My Results

They say you shall know a tree by the fruit that it bears. So is my Rock, Paper, Scissors philosophy really producing any fruit? I will let you read for yourself my major successes that happened in within the last year. This was a crazy year for me and my team!

---

## Verizon Wireless Everyday Hero Award

I have won the Verizon Wireless Everyday Hero Award recognizing me for my schools programs and motivational speeches. Several Verizon executives flew here and had a banquet for me and other semi finalists and I was awarded a tablet, cash reward, and a store voucher where I bought 2 brand new iphones. They also recorded an interview of me and posted it on their website. Pretty cool if you ask me...

## Saint Louis Connect Care Promoting Teen Excellence

I won an award for promoting teen excellence in my city. I was given a trophy, and a proclamation from the Saint Louis Tax Bureau. I was number 1 out of 4 award recipients including Hall of Famer Lou Brock, Judge Jimmie Edwards, and Dr. Whittico who is a local legendary physician in Saint Louis.

## Major Contracts Expanded Across Saint Louis

I expanded my visions reach by solidifying 3 major school districts to contract me for my services. Most of them committed to a yearly renewal.

## Partnered With Opera Theatre STL and Grammy Jazz Musician Terence Blanchard

I was thrilled with the opportunity to partner with the prestigious Opera Theatre and world renowned jazz great Terence Blanchard for his upcoming play debut called Champion. Terence Blanchard helped artist develop some of my best students in the world at Lee Hamilton Elementary. Students recorded at my studio with media cameras rolling. This is what life is all about. Giving kids an opportunity that I didn't have growing up.

## Feature Story on PBS and NBC

Two feature stories on my business. One on PBS with Emmy Award winner Ruth Ezell for the Terence Blanchard story, and the other from working with the students at Confluence Academy.

## Office Depot Foundation

I received an all expense paid trip to be interviewed for the opportunity to tour over 300 schools as a part of an anti-bullying campaign endorsed by the world wide super group One Direction.

## Gateway Classic Foundation

I had the great privilege to speak at The Gateway Classic Gala and walk on the field to present over $80,000 in full ride scholarships to students. I saw myself on the first jumbo-tron.

## Walgreens Expressions Challenge Partnership

We contracted as a spokesperson for the Walgreens Expressions Challenge. My first regional contract encouraging kids to make artistic positive self expressions.

## Saint Louis Rams

The Saint Louis Rams corporate outreach department decided to clear the office and come see me speak with the intentions on partnering in 2014. I rarely get nervous when I speak, but this time I sweated a little.

## Humanitarian Of The Year: Traffic Music Awards 2014

It was announced in the summer of 2013 that I won this award for 2014. The traffic music awards is the Who's Who list for our community artists and movers and shakers.

## Spoke to over 10,000 students in 2013

I have spoke to over 10,000 students in 2013. That's 10,000 people I wouldn't have touched if I would have given up. Your mission is bigger than you, remember?

## Cadillac Magazine Ad

Cadillac along with Saint Louis Mag decided to salute my wife and I for our outreach to schools. This featured ad was our first magazine, and it blew my mind when I first saw it on the news stands.

## Never Give Up

It's amazing how despite all the pressure I felt to give up, I stayed rooted and grounded in my mission statement long enough to see the light at the end of the tunnel. In less than one year, I had the most successful year ever. What if I would have quit and went back to work? All I had to do was stay focused and keep pushing. I have learned when the pressure is on to the point where you feel like giving up and quitting, do not give up. All you have to do is look at your victory board and meditate on just how mentally strong you are. Thanksgiving is one of the most powerful forces you possess as humans. In your lowest moments find ways to think thankful thoughts. Whenever you hit a valley moment in your life, thanksgiving sends powerful vibes throughout the universe that proclaims and indicates through faith that a big breakthrough is right around the corner. See your way out of adversity always because you are not average!

---

"The greater danger for most of us is not that our aim is too high and we miss it, but that we aim too low and we reach it."
-Michelangelo Buonarroti

---

# CHAPTER 23
# FINAL THOUGHTS

"You can't change the world sitting from the comfort
of your own couch." -Author Unknown

There are so many more amazing stories that I would like to
share with you, but hopefully you have got the point on how
to properly achieve success by now. I would like to thank
every person who has bought my book from the bottom of
my heart. It has been a pleasure to have shared with you all
the many struggles I have overcome with the hopes that the
child like dreamer inside you would be awakened! There is
no such thing as the word impossible. Most of these stories
where birthed in my mind as possibilities in spite of
everything around me saying that things were impossible. I

am now a true testament that you can think your way out of debt, lack, poverty, ignorance, and defeat if you develop the will power to be hopeful and expect the best in every situation. I once heard a wise man say that success is going from failure to failure without losing enthusiasm. Don't let the troubles of the world toss you around like a boat without the sail. Your words have power which is magnetized by your mindset. If you expect the worst, you will receive the worst. If you expect the best, you will receive the best. Even in times of extreme doubt, lift up your head and speak to the mountains of adversity and watch them be removed through faith and patience.

---

### So What's Next?

When moving up the ladder of success, it's always best to take note of the people who went before you. Billy Graham, a world renowned preacher who lead millions of people to salvation, once said if he could do it all over again he would have spent more time with his family and been a little more compassionate with people about their flaws.

In 2013, I chased and desired success and while success is good, it cannot fill the void you may have in your life. Only love can do that. There have been so many moments on my pursuit to change the world and live my dream that I got off the path. The burdens of life made it hard to move forward. The Bowser in me sucked the life out of dreams and although I was moving forward with progress, my love and passion for serving the community became dry and stale. Listening to others around me instead of my inner voice made me start to lust for the money, fame, positioning, and power. I can assure you, this is not where you want to be.

Too much business can cloud your vision and you will feel like a slave to the dream.

## Ferguson Missouri

On Aug 9, 2014 I was sitting on the couch thumbing through one of my social media timelines. I always see many things happening in the world in real time from the media posts, but this time I saw an unusual number of posts about a young African American male who had been shot by a Ferguson police officer in the Canfield Green apartment complex. My eyes were stunned and my heart cried out, as I started to see a heavy flow of pictures being posted of this young man laying dead on the ground with no ambulance in site. I decided to put my phone down and take a break from the news that gave me deep sorrows to my heart, but when I picked up my phone again, there were posts all the way down my timeline from everybody in my friends list showing the young man still laying on the ground without any medical assistance.

The next few hours became devastating to my city. The citizens became outraged after hearing that the young man was shot several times even though he was unarmed and his hands were in the air in the surrender position. Hearing the cries of a mother seeing her helpless son's body laying on the ground at the hands of Ferguson police officer on the ground for 4 hours in the heat grew anger and frustration in the crowd.

Then to make matters worse, the police were seen on video pulling up in the community with riot gear and M-16s locked and loaded and ready to shoot. This simple act of force angered the crowd even more. They felt as if the police who had been harassing them all this time had finally committed the unforgivable sin, and they were ready to war against the police at all cost.

Soon after, the local and the major media outlets had now caught wind of what had happened, and over the next few days as the crowds filled the streets of Ferguson, Missouri to protest the fact that a police officer had gunned down an unarmed teen and was not put into custody while receiving paid administrative leave. The strip filled daily with thousands of people chanting, "Hands up, don't shoot," as a symbolism for justice for unarmed teen Michael Brown.

Over the next few days, there was a heavy cloud of depression and weariness that covered my city. Most African American males I know had all experienced some form of police brutality or excessive force, but we all felt that there was nothing we could do about it. Coming from urban America, oppression from poverty and heavy incarcerations had become so frequent that we had accepted abuse as a norm of life. But this frustration did not go away, it only became a breeding ground for violence, gangs, black on black crime, drug infested neighborhoods, and a high incarceration rate which leads to fatherless homes and community division. It was if my entire city had stopped and finally said that enough is enough, it's time to fight back and stand up for justice.

Over the next few days, the story of Mike Browns shooting had now been heard around the world with 24 hours live broadcast displaying a swarm of police officers dressed in riot gear pulling up in tanks pointed at the crowd. As camera crews from all over the world watched the live standoff of hundreds of police officers angered protestors, this crazy ordeal ended with hundreds arrested, businesses set on fire, tear gas fired and rubber bullets shot at peaceful protestors by the police, and a city left in an unbelievable uproar of hatred.

## Be Heard

"Our lives begin to end the day we become silent about things that matter." -Martin Luther King Jr.

I as well as others across the world, could not believe what we were witnessing. A small peaceful town had turned into a war zone similar to Iraq in a matter of hours. So why am I writing this story at the end of my book? I truly believe that the Mike Brown situation is a wake up call for America for those who are called to lead. Now more than ever, we need young leaders to stand up and fix the division problem that we have in our country. Millennials are honestly tired of turning on the news and seeing democrats and republicans fight against each other and spend millions of dollars on smear campaign ads against their opponents. Even stats show that if you run too many negative ads against your opponents that it starts to make the person running the ads look bad. Do you know why? We are tired of being a nation divided. We are tired of the world asking for our votes but ignore our request for mentoring and collaboration across all ethnic groups. We are crying out for help and refuse to be ignored. We want the right to be heard, valued, and respected no matter our age.

"If you want to change Saint Louis, change yourself. If you want to blame Saint Louis, blame yourself." -Koran Bolden

## My Solution

Dream so big that people laugh at you, but then take as
many risks as possible until you achieve success. As you
begin to build an award winning empire using the principles
in this book, please remember to stay humble through it all
as arrogance and pride can blind the most talented people in
the world to walk in a pitfall. Be good enough in your mind to
know where you're going, but not too good that you forget
where you came from. When I started my business, I was
asking for every man I met to mentor me and put me in the
game. Some of them helped temporarily while others
rejected me all together. The anger and frustration from the
lack of help had me bitter but I had to get over it fast and
understand my calling. Sometimes we pray and ask to be a
great leader and to be used mightily to change the world but
don't quite understand what it is that we are asking for.
When you want to be great, you are asking to be tested and
tried to be a helpless vessel of service. By going through all
the rejection, I can now comfort those that have been
rejected. Through making mistakes, I am now qualified to
empower those that have made mistakes. It's almost like
being in the army. After you have won all the battles you gain
the stripes needed for respect and honor. As a Millennial, I
know that my turn to be the youngest in charge is coming.
After years of self discipline and overcoming hardship, I am
gaining the patience to weather any storm which is why most
people give up on their dreams. They lack the patience to
see it through.

## From Me To We

---

"When I stand before God at the end of my life, I would hope that I would not have a single bit of talent left and could say, I used everything you gave me." –Erma Bombeck

---

Moving forward, my goal is to build up the next group of business leaders. We will prepare ourselves to influence the world with our love, finances, and resources. Our outreach will be like no other since the beginning of time. If we dare come together and put all of our differences to the side for the sake of our youth, we can achieve the impossible. We will walk in integrity and be clothed in humility but are unapologetic and enthusiastic when we say that we will be the youngest in charge. We plan to change the world without asking for anyone's permission because that goal is not up for negotiation because we have our Rock, Paper, and Scissors.

"The question isn't who is going to let me;
It's who is going to stop me." -Ayn Rand

---

"The question isn't who is going to let us;
It's who is going to stop us." -Koran Bolden

## *I Wanted To Change The World*

*When I was a young man, I wanted to change the world.*

*I found it was difficult to change the world, so I tried to change my nation.*

*When I found I couldn't change the nation, I began to focus on my town. I couldn't change the town and as an older man, I tried to change my family.*

*Now, as an old man, I realize the only thing I can change is myself, and suddenly I realize that if long ago I had changed myself, I could have made an impact on my family. My family and I could have made an impact on our town. Their impact could have changed the nation and I could indeed have changed the world.*

*Author: unknown monk around 1100 AD*

# About The Author

Koran Bolden is a national youth motivational speaker and CEO of Street Dreamz Recording Studio and Party Center. He is the recent recipient of the Verizon Wireless Everyday Hero award, the Cadillac City Shapers Salute, and spokesperson for the regional Walgreens Expressions Challenge. Bolden and his wife LaPortcia, strive to support and empower students to make healthy life choices to graduate from school on time. After influencing over 30,000 people and being featured in several media outlets, they were inspired to recently open satellite Street Dreamz School of Business and Performing Arts Centers in various schools across the country that focuses on leadership, character education, conflict resolution, business, and entrepreneurship through the arts. They currently reside in Saint Louis, MO with their 3 children, Koran Jr, Tahlia, and Kailee.

# KORAN BOLDEN
### National Youth Speaker & Entrepreneur

## ROCK PAPER
## SCISSORS

3 SECRETS TO HOW YOUR
FAILURES CAN MAKE YOU
# FAMOUS

### Business Strategy for Millennials

Online Dream Success Classes Starting Soon!
www.KoranBolden.com